Praise for *Service Learning in the PreK–3 Classroom*:

"Young children get excited and deeply engaged when they have opportunities to do real work, solve meaningful and interesting problems, and, in the process, gain expertise about the world around them. *Service Learning in the PreK–3 Classroom* is a wonderfully comprehensive and incredibly practical resource that offers teachers guidance about how to create these opportunities in their classrooms. The book includes everything teachers will need to implement projects—from the theoretical underpinnings, to the standards addressed, to the reproducible forms. I am excited to share this rich and innovative new resource with the educators with whom I work."
—**Judy Jablon, educational consultant and author of** *Powerful Interactions: How to Connect with Children to Extend Their Learning* **(NAEYC)**

"At last there is a practical resource specifically designed to help preK–3 teachers integrate service learning into their pedagogy! Lake and Jones have crafted a wonderfully useful guide that includes service learning definitions, national standards, examples, planning tools, lesson plans, and a gold mine of grab-and-go forms and reproducibles. Grounded in learning and developmental theory yet focused on practice, this new how-to guide belongs on the shelf of every preK–3 teacher interested in bringing learning to life through service."
—**Joe Follman, founding director, Florida Learn & Serve**

"Young children have an inherent concern for their world. Teachers can respond by engaging them in meaningful acts through service learning. *Service Learning in the PreK–3 Classroom* is a helpful guide for educators who want to ensure that our youngest participants have opportunities to contribute to society."
—**Cathryn Berger Kaye, M.A., author of** *The Complete Guide to Service Learning*

"Caring starts early and, if we are fortunate, continues throughout our lives. This book is a great resource for educators to embrace their critical role in shaping the mindset of young students and teaching them that *others matter.* Lake and Jones have created a detailed map to a wonderful destination."
—**Clifton L. Taulbert, K–12 education consultant and author of** *Eight Habits of the Heart for Educators*

"This book is a vital resource for early childhood educators—including classroom teachers, preservice teachers, and teacher educators. The comprehensiveness combined with the remarkably clear way of communicating how to use service learning as a methodology make this book a required resource for anyone who wants to link experiential learning with the development of social responsibility. This book is filled with real-life examples, organizational resources, and theoretical support that will provide valuable assistance and time-saving tools, which are teachers' best friends."
—**Elizabeth A. Ethridge, Ed.D., associate professor of early childhood education, University of Oklahoma**

Service Learning
in the PreK–3 Classroom

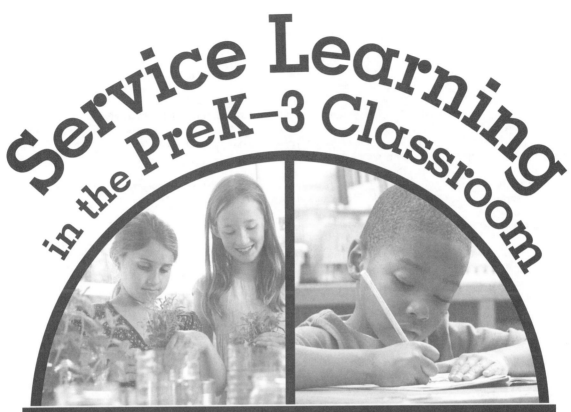

The What, Why, and How-To Guide for Every Teacher

Vickie E. Lake, Ph.D., and Ithel Jones, Ed.D.

free spirit
PUBLISHING®

Copyright © 2012 by Vickie E. Lake, Ph.D., and Ithel Jones, Ed.D.

Library of Congress Cataloging-in-Publication Data
Lake, Vickie E.
 Service learning in the Prek-3 classroom : the what, why, and how-to guide for every teacher / by Vickie E. Lake and Ithel Jones.
  p. cm.
 ISBN 978-1-57542-367-8
1. Service learning—Study and teaching (Early childhood)—United States. 2. Service learning—Study and teaching (Elementary)—United States. 3. Service learning—United States—Curricula. I. Jones, Ithel. II. Title.
LC220.5.L35 2012
372.8—dc23

                                                        2011046353

eBook ISBN: 978-1-57542-679-2

Free Spirit Publishing does not have control over or assume responsibility for author or third-party websites and their content. At the time of this book's publication, all facts and figures cited within are the most current available. All telephone numbers, addresses, and website URLs are accurate and active; all publications, organizations, websites, and other resources exist as described in this book; and all have been verified as of August 2011. If you find an error or believe that a resource listed here is not as described, please contact Free Spirit Publishing. Parents, teachers, and other adults: We strongly urge you to monitor children's use of the Internet.

Edited by Meg Bratsch
Cover and interior design by Michelle Lee
Illustrations by Michelle Lee

Leaf illustration © istockphoto.com/jangeltun
Cover photos, clockwise from top right: Wealan Pollard/OJO Images/Jupiterimages; Image Source/the Agency Collection/Getty Images; SW Productions/Photodisc/Getty Images; Milk & Honey Creative/Brand X Pictures/Getty Images
Photo, page 4: Milk & Honey Creative/Brand X Pictures/Jupiterimages
Photo, page 116: Image Source/the Agency Collection/Jupiterimages
Headline font on kids' repro pages by Denise Bentulan

10 9 8 7 6 5 4 3 2 1
Printed in the United States of America

Free Spirit Publishing Inc.
Minneapolis, MN
(612) 338-2068
help4kids@freespirit.com
www.freespirit.com

Dedication

I dedicate this book to Fairye, my mother and friend.
Vickie Lake

I dedicate this book to my wife Gill, and my two children, Megan and Dylan,
for their support and unconditional love. I also dedicate this book to the memory of my mother,
who provided the early inspiration to continue learning.
Ithel Jones

Acknowledgments

Many people have influenced our thinking and understanding about service learning in early childhood education. This book is the product of almost four years of research, product development, and writing. During this time we've worked with hundreds of preservice and in-service teachers to provide them with the knowledge, skills, and dispositions to successfully implement service learning projects with young children. Each of these individuals has helped shape our ideas about service learning in early childhood education. The preservice teachers in particular have allowed us to field-test our ideas, and have collaborated with us to design exciting new projects for students. We are extremely grateful to each and every one of the preservice teachers we have worked with, many of whom are quoted in the sample lessons throughout this book.

We are also fortunate to have the ongoing cooperation and support of a large group of early childhood teachers. Some of these teachers have collaborated with our early childhood program for more than two decades. The work and examples described in this text would not have been possible without the support of these teachers. Thanks also to the administrators, staff, and parents at the following Leon County elementary schools: Woodville, Springwood, Kate Sullivan, Hawks Rise, DeSoto Trails, Buck Lake, and Canopy Oaks.

This book would not have been possible without the active help and encouragement of the following graduate students: Brooke Klett, Cassie Frost, Susan Silverman, Suzanne Adinolfi, Tiffany McMonigle, Erin Hinojosa, and Lori Kelly.

We are also grateful to the following people for supporting our work on service learning with young children: Joe Follman, former director, Florida Learn & Serve, Florida State University; The Corporation for National and Community Service; and The College of Education, Florida State University.

Finally, we extend our thanks and appreciation to the staff of Free Spirit Publishing for their vision and perseverance, notably publisher Judy Galbraith, editor Meg Bratsch, and designer Michelle Lee.

Contents

Part One: Service Learning in Early Childhood—A Primer

2 Part Two: Project Forms and Templates

Part Three: Sample Lesson Plans

Part Four: Supporting Research and Teacher Education

List of Reproducible Forms

Chapter 5

Chapter 6

Chapter 7

Chapter 8

Chapter 14

CD-ROM Contents

- All reproducible forms from the book (as customizable PDFs)

- *Service Learning in the PreK–3 Classroom* PowerPoint presentation

Introduction

Following is the story of a service learning project titled "Sunshine in a Pot," completed by a group of students in preschool, kindergarten, and first grade. With the help of two teachers, the children grew flowers from seeds, planted them in pots they decorated, made greeting cards, and delivered the cards and flower pots to patients in a local hospital. In the process, the students learned about a plant's parts and life cycle, about human illness and injuries, and about empathy. Following are the words of one of the teachers reflecting back on the project.

Sunshine in a Pot

"Before we began the activity, I explained to the students that we would be helping others by spreading a little sunshine through the gift of a potted flower. We discussed the local hospital and the reasons why people had to stay there: sickness, injuries, cancer, pregnancy, etc. We also talked about how sad it can be at the hospital because you aren't at home with your family and usually you aren't feeling well. The students were able to participate in the conversation and many discussed situations where their own family members had been in the hospital.

"After our lengthy discussion, I told the students that they would be painting a pot and planting a flower in it for someone in the hospital who was ill or injured. The students asked if they would be taking the pots to the hospital themselves, and I explained that I would be taking the pots there after school. I asked the students, 'Do you think the patients will like getting a gift like this in the hospital?' All the students said yes, and one student said, 'We sent flowers to my grandmother when she was in the hospital, and she liked them.'

"The students seemed very interested in the activity and everyone did a wonderful job painting their pots very colorfully. We planted pretty purple flowers called Hawaii Blues. The activity took the entire day to complete because we worked in small groups. They painted the pots in the morning and planted the flowers in the afternoon. I was very surprised that no one asked to take theirs home; this showed they understood the reason for the activity, which was helping others."
—*Ashley and Dawn, preservice teachers of preschool through first grade, Tallahassee, Florida*

In their own reflections on the project, here are examples of what the students had to say:

- "We need to be nice to people who are sick."
- "Giving someone a present can make them feel better."
- "We made people feel better by giving them the pot and flower."
- "We made cards for them, too. My card said, 'Happy Spring and Get Well Soon.'"
- "We had fun making a present for someone who is sick."
- "It made sick people smile, because someone cared about them."

It is clear from this example that service learning can be a powerful tool in reaching, teaching, and inspiring young children. In this modern, rapidly changing world, quality early education is essential for our students' future success. This success is defined not only in academic terms but also from a social, civic, and moral perspective. Thus, teachers need opportunities to enrich children's learning that support high academic standards and, at the same time, foster children's social development by teaching them to be good citizens. The methodology of service learning offers teachers these opportunities.

In recent years, service learning has gained a strong foothold in middle grade and secondary classrooms, and it is time to employ its many rich benefits at the early childhood level. Our goal in writing this book is to provide you, as a preK or primary grade educator, with a solid understanding of how service learning can be effectively used with young children. We also aim to help you see the connections between the philosophical basis of service learning and the practice of service learning. To this end, we have included a theoretical rationale for service learning in early childhood, as well as stories from a variety of classrooms in which 215 preservice teachers in our Florida State University program conducted field trials with over 3,500 students in preschool through grade three. These stories serve to highlight how teachers and programs can integrate service learning into applied practice, aligning with academic learning standards in all content areas while providing developmentally appropriate experiences for young children. The wealth of examples of tried-and-tested projects demonstrates how service learning meets the needs of young children in developmentally appropriate ways; in short, they show meaningful early childhood learning at its best.

Service Learning in the PreK–3 Classroom is also intended for those who work with you on all levels—administrators, counselors, parents, members of a professional learning community, preservice teachers, college faculty, and others. Simply put, it is for education professionals and students everywhere who seek a better understanding of service learning and its role in the early childhood classroom. The book is subtitled *The What, Why, and How-To Guide* because its practical approach develops the background knowledge and skills you need to effectively use service learning as pedagogy in programs for young children.

About This Book

The text is organized into four parts: the first part explains what service learning is and can accomplish; the second part provides tools and templates for implementing service learning in the classroom;

> The wealth of examples of tried-and-tested projects demonstrates how service learning meets the needs of young children in developmentally appropriate ways; in short, they show meaningful early childhood learning at its best.

the third part shows examples of service learning projects that have been carried out with all ages of young children; and the final part describes how service learning is rooted in solid academic theory and can be used as part of a teacher education or professional development program.

Part One: Service Learning in Early Childhood—A Primer addresses the background and purpose (the "what" and "why") of service learning in early childhood education. It provides you with a context in which to learn about the reasons for doing service with young children and guidelines for implementation.

Chapter 1 defines service learning and outlines the principles and standards upon which it is based. In **Chapter 2,** you will read an overview of the theoretical rationale for using service learning with young children, as well as how the practice supports character education, differentiated instruction, and other important classroom initiatives. **Chapter 3** outlines how service learning in the early grades can support high academic standards as outlined in national and state policies and documents. In **Chapter 4,** we recommend how to effectively design service learning for early childhood programs, no matter what your prior knowledge of or experience with the practice.

In **Part Two: Project Forms and Templates**, we address more specifically the "how" of service learning by providing tools for designing and evaluating service learning projects with young children. **Chapter 5** includes forms and templates for introducing, brainstorming, planning, preparing, and organizing projects. **Chapter 6** provides the necessary documents to use when working with community partners. Ideas and activities for reflecting on and documenting a service learning experience are found in **Chapter 7**. And **Chapter**

8 offers several important assessment and evaluation forms to use with all project participants, both children and adults.

Part Three: Sample Lesson Plans and Resources is filled with memorable snapshots of service learning in practice. Here you will read about richly varied examples of projects that the preservice teachers in our university program have successfully completed in hundreds of early childhood classrooms throughout the Tallahassee, Florida, region. This section is organized around four themes that we have found to be particularly useful in the early grades: **Chapter 9**: Letter Writing, **Chapter 10**: Gardening, **Chapter 11**: Helping Others, and **Chapter 12**: Environmental Issues. These examples of artifacts from a range of actual projects help provide a complete ground-level view of service learning for early childhood educators. Page 162 includes a matrix listing all sample lesson plans by topic, grade level, and subject area, along with additional project ideas. Pages 205–207 include children's book and website recommendations that correspond to the lesson plans.

Finally, **Part Four: Supporting Research and Teacher Education** discusses in more detail the theoretical support for service learning with young children (**Chapter 13**). Finally, and importantly, it discusses how to incorporate service learning into early childhood teachers' professional development and teacher education programs (**Chapter 14**), because successful implementation of service learning projects ultimately depends on the teacher.

In addition, the **CD-ROM** includes a PowerPoint presentation that gives a comprehensive overview of the service learning process and highlights the benefits and rationales for using service learning in early childhood classrooms. It also contains all the forms and templates from the book as downloadable, customizable, and printable PDF files.

How to Use This Book

We hope this book will serve as a catalyst for you to begin using service learning. If you are a classroom teacher who is new to service learning, you may wish to read the book straight through, selecting advice, guidelines, and project examples to follow based on your individual needs. If you

have some prior experience with the practice, you can pick and choose those sections relevant to your early childhood program and make a list of new methods, ideas, and forms to try. You may also wish to share the book or specific sections of it with members of your professional learning community, if you participate in one. If you're a teacher educator, you might want your students or participants to read selected chapters that correspond with your course or training goals and objectives. This book can serve as an additional scaffold for your students as you work with them in the area of service learning.

At a minimum, by studying the practical examples the book provides, you will see how service learning builds on children's interests, motivation, and learning in all subject areas. These highly effective projects were all designed and implemented by novice teachers. Thus, even if you have limited experience in using a service learning approach, you can draw on a wide range of resources, including those in this book, to provide a curriculum enriched with service learning. As you begin designing your own projects, use the book's practical, concrete suggestions for evaluating their effectiveness. Whether you are a new or an experienced teacher of young children, this guide will help you reconceptualize your curriculum to include truly meaningful learning.

Ultimately, we created this book to share our successes in developing and implementing service learning projects in early childhood classrooms. The work of the committed teachers and school leaders with whom we have partnered deserves to be recognized and celebrated. We share their stories and projects to help support educators like you who want to enrich the learning experiences of their young students. These pages are full of ideas to think about—including teachers' stories to draw inspiration from, lesson plans and activities to implement, lists of invaluable websites and books, and other resources to turn to for information and assistance. We hope you will use this book to create and fulfill your own vision of how service learning can be used to make a difference in the lives of your students and community members alike.

Vickie E. Lake, Ph.D., and Ithel Jones, Ed.D.

PART ONE

Service Learning in Early Childhood— A Primer

Chapter 1

What Is Service Learning?

Kindergarten students design posters to encourage others not to litter. A class of second-grade students arranges a fund-raising event for victims of a hurricane. Preschool children plant flowers in their school garden to beautify their school's campus. All are examples of service learning in childhood education. Service learning, with its emphasis on connecting school curriculum with service projects that address real needs, is widely recognized as a meaningful and effective approach for teaching children.

This chapter defines service learning and discusses the principles upon which it is based. It also presents the current standards and indicators for quality practice and examines the various approaches to and formal stages of service learning.

Service Learning Defined

Service learning can be viewed as both an instructional approach and a philosophy of learning.

An Instructional Approach

According to the Corporation for National and Community Service (CNCS), a federally funded U.S. agency has supported service learning combines service to the community with student learning in a way that improves both the student and the community. More specifically, service learning:

- is a method whereby students learn and develop through active participation in thoughtfully organized service that is conducted in and meets the needs of communities

- is coordinated with a preschool, elementary school, secondary school, institution of higher education, or community service program and the community

- helps foster civic responsibility

- is integrated into and enhances the academic curriculum of the students, or the education components of the community service program in which the participants are enrolled

- provides structured time for students or participants to reflect on the service experience

During the past two decades, service learning has increased in popularity in the United States. It is estimated, for example, that in the 2007–2008 academic year more than 4.2 million students were involved in some type of service learning or service activity.[1] Given the large number of students involved, it is inevitable that not everyone will use the same definition of service learning. Yet, despite the wide range of interpretations, Learn and Serve America has succeeded in capturing its essence:

> **Service learning** combines service objectives with learning objectives with the intent that the activity changes both the recipient and the provider of the service. This is accomplished by combining service tasks with structured opportunities that link the task to self-reflection, self-discovery, and the acquisition and comprehension of values, skills, and knowledge content.[2]

---

[1] Spring, K., Grimm, R., & Dietz, N. (2009)
[2] Learn and Serve America (2007)

This definition of service learning represents the core concept upon which the approach is based. The educational value of service learning stems from the fact that, in the words of author and expert Cathryn Berger Kaye, "it connects school-based curriculum with the inherent caring and concern young people have for their world."[3] It is through this integration of service and classroom content that students develop a deeper understanding of content, leading to improved academic learning. Simply put, a service learning approach makes learning meaningful for children.

Federal Support

Recently, federal support for service learning has increased in the United States, under the National and Community Service Trust Act of 1993 and the revised Serve America Act of 2009. Among the stated purposes of the Serve America Act are the following:

- meet the unmet human, educational, environmental, and public safety needs of the United States, without displacing workers

- renew the ethic of civic responsibility and the spirit of community throughout the United States

- expand educational opportunity by rewarding individuals who participate in national service with an increased ability to pursue higher education or job training

- encourage citizens of the United States, regardless of age, income, or disability, to engage in full-time or part-time national service

- provide tangible benefits to the communities in which national service is performed

- expand and strengthen service learning programs through year-round opportunities to improve the education of children and teens and to maximize the benefits of national and community service

- focus national service on the areas of national need such service has the capacity to address, such as improving education, increasing energy conservation, improving the health status of economically disadvantaged individuals, and

improving economic opportunity for economically disadvantaged individuals[4]

Additionally, support for service learning is evident in the No Child Left Behind Act (2001). This legislation offers federal funding for character education programs, which can include service learning. These programs include educating children about caring, citizenship, fairness, respect, and responsibility, which mirror the six pillars of character according to Character Counts, a national program of Josephson Institute, a nonprofit organization.

Unfortunately, on April 8, 2011, the U.S. Congress made substantial funding cuts for the Corporation for National and Community Service and eliminated funding altogether for its program Learn and Serve America, which provides research, training, technical support, and grant money to schools and community organizations involved in service learning. However, many people are campaigning to reinstate, and even increase, funding for the CNCS and Learn and Serve America.[5] In addition, service learning continues to grow at a rapid pace in schools and districts throughout the United States, as more than half of the states have adopted policies that both support and regulate its practice.

> Those who promote a service learning approach believe that education should include the development of social responsibility.

A Philosophy of Learning

In addition to being an increasingly popular instructional approach, service learning can be described as a philosophy of learning. Those who promote a service learning approach believe that education should include the development of social responsibility, and that the most effective learning is active and connected to experience in some way. Service learning programs are explicitly structured so that students learn

[3] Kaye (2010), p. 8
[4] Serve America Act (2009), Public Law 111-113, p. 6–8.
[5] You can join the campaign "Save Service in America" here: saveservice.org.

about the larger social issues behind the problems they are addressing through service, including the historical, economic, cultural, and political contexts involved.

Service Learning Standards

Because of the emphasis on student learning, it is hardly surprising that educators, researchers, and others have consistently called for high quality in service learning. Quality is important in order to ensure that service learning lives up to its promise of positive outcomes. Until recently, determining quality in service learning was difficult because of the lack of consensus on what constitutes quality practice. With the publication of official standards in 2008, quality in service learning can now be easily determined.

The 10 principles listed below influenced these standards, which were developed through an extensive national consultation process involving students, teachers, school and district administrators, community members, staff from community-based organizations, policy makers, and others interested in service learning. Drawing on extensive research and the professional judgment of key stakeholders, the eight standards and 35 indicators provide a common set of well-defined and measurable expectations for high quality practice. (See pages 202–203 for a complete list of the standards and indicators.)

The Principles of Service Learning

In May 1989, The Johnson Foundation at Wingspread, an organization committed to sustainable environmental and community solutions, hosted an advisory group meeting that developed 10 Principles of Good Practice for Combining Service and Learning. This group consolidated information from extensive consultations with more than 70 organizations interested or involved in service and learning. These principles, still used today, are summarized as follows.

Service Learning . . .

1. **Engages** people in responsible and challenging actions for the common good.

2. **Provides** structured opportunities for people to reflect critically on their service experience.

3. **Articulates** clear service and learning goals for everyone involved.

4. **Allows** for those with needs to define those needs.

5. **Clarifies** the responsibilities of each person and organization involved.

6. **Matches** service providers and service needs through a process that recognizes changing circumstances.

7. **Expects** genuine, active, and sustained organizational commitment.

8. **Includes** training, supervision, monitoring, support, recognition, and evaluation to meet service and learning goals.

9. **Insures** that the time commitment for service and learning is flexible, appropriate, and in the best interests of all involved.

10. **Commits** to program participation by and with diverse populations.

Service Learning Standards for Quality Practice[6]

1. **Meaningful Service.** Service learning actively engages participants in meaningful and personally relevant activities.

2. **Link to Curriculum**. Service learning is intentionally used as an instructional strategy to meet learning goals and/or content standards.

3. **Reflection.** Service learning incorporates multiple challenging reflection activities that are ongoing and that prompt deep thinking and analysis about oneself and one's relationship to society.

4. **Diversity.** Service learning promotes understanding of diversity and mutual respect among all participants.

5. **Youth Voice.** Service learning provides students with a strong voice in planning, implementing, and evaluating service learning experiences with guidance from adults.

6. **Partnerships**. Service learning partnerships are collaborative, mutually beneficial, and address community needs.

7. **Progress Monitoring.** Service learning engages participants in an ongoing process to assess the quality of implementation and progress toward meeting specified goals, and uses results for improvement and sustainability.

8. **Duration and Intensity**. Service learning has sufficient duration and intensity to address community needs and meet specified outcomes.

Components of Service Learning

"Through service learning, the often elusive idea of 'community' takes shape and has a more tangible meaning for all involved," according to expert author Cathryn Berger Kaye.[7] The term *community* is defined in two ways: geographically and socially. How we define community in service learning depends on the nature of the activity. For example, in the context of teacher education courses, community could be defined as one classroom or several classrooms, a school or campus, the immediate surroundings of a school or campus, a town, a region, a state, a nation, or globally. Depending on the community and the nature of the activity, a service learning project is classified as one of four different approaches, described as follows.

The Four Approaches to Service Learning[8]

1. **Direct Service.** Students' service directly affects and involves the recipients face-to-face.

2. **Indirect Service.** Students do not provide service to an individual but to the community as a whole and may not meet the recipients in person.

3. **Advocacy.** Students' intent is to create awareness of or promote action on an issue of public interest.

4. **Research.** Students find, gather, and report on information in the public interest.

Based on these approaches, service learning can look similar to community service. However, while the extent to which they are similar will depend on the type of service learning project, Kaye stresses that community service and service learning are different, as you will discover in the following section.

The Five Stages of Service Learning

Service learning has five interdependent stages: investigation, preparation, action, reflection, and documentation. These stages are what makes service learning very distinct from community service, which typically begins with action and may or may not include reflection or demonstration.

Stage 1: Investigation

Every project begins with investigation. You and your students work together to investigate and learn about the issues in your community, discover your strengths and abilities, and identify a need to address. This need might emerge from books, curriculum, the Internet, personal observations and experiences, surveys, interviews, or discussions.

[6] National Youth Leadership Council (2008), www.nylc.org. Reprinted with permission.
[7] Kaye (2010), p. 10
[8] ibid., p. 11

Stage 2: Preparation

Once the community need is addressed, you and your students prepare for action. Preparation involves looking into the need more in-depth, finding out what others have done and are doing to address the need, seeking out partners (such as other classrooms, people with particular skills, or local or national agencies), collecting materials and resources, and creating an action plan.

Stage 3: Action

The third stage, action, is the direct result of preparation. The action plan is carried out over time—a day, a week, a semester, a year. During the action stage, you and your students continue to develop knowledge and resources. The children experience the real-world results of their plan, observe their strengths and abilities in relation to others, and develop an appreciation for collaborative effort.

It is at this point that community service and service learning part ways. The cycle for community service is investigation, preparation, and action. However, in order for an activity or project to be considered service learning, two more critical stages must be included: *reflection* and *demonstration*.

Stage 4: Reflection

Reflection is a vital and ongoing process in service learning and integrates learning and experience with personal growth and awareness. Your students consider how the experience, knowledge, and skills they are acquiring relate to their own lives. They put the experience into the larger community context, while you encourage them to be creative and use multiple intelligences in their reflections. Effective service learning teachers instigate this reflection by giving students assignments that require them to talk about, write about,

> While their approaches can look similar, community service and service learning are different.

make drawings of, and evaluate their activities and impacts. Such assignments deepen students' understanding and provide avenues for teachers to assess what students have learned and accomplished.

Stage 5: Demonstration

Demonstration is the final stage and it both adds to the service and learning involved in the project and provides evidence of what your students have gained and accomplished through their experience. The children demonstrate what they have learned by teaching or otherwise sharing with others about the needs they have addressed, the activities they have conducted, and the impacts they have had. Demonstration activities (as in the reflection stage, these activities are often assignments) can be for audiences outside of the classroom and can include student presentations, talks, lessons, exhibits, drawings, writings, public art, letters, public service announcements, performances, poetry, and more.

Chapter Summary

Service learning is an approach that enables children to learn through active participation in organized service. By using service learning as a pedagogy, you help foster civic responsibility in your students. Service learning also enhances the academic curriculum by fostering a deeper understanding of the material and by making the learning more meaningful to students.

Chapter 2

Why Use Service Learning with Young Children?

Service learning, as described in Chapter 1, is an instructional approach that is known to benefit students of all ages. Educators at the middle and high school levels have long recognized the value of service learning as pedagogy. We now know that service learning is also a powerful and effective approach in the education of young children—between the ages of three and eight, or preschool to grade three.

The power of service learning is evident in the words of this early childhood preservice teacher who completed a service learning project in which kindergarten students supported victims of Hurricane Katrina in 2005.

"Through the 'Hurricane Relief' service learning project, my students benefited because now they are aware of the problems and dangers of natural disasters like hurricanes. They are aware that people and families outside of our city are going through troubles, and that these people need support and friendship from others. They learned how to be a good friend to people they have never met before. My students' knowledge has changed because they are now aware of new things. There were actually students who didn't know what a hurricane was, so they learned what a hurricane looks like (through books) and about the strong winds and rain. All the students learned what could happen if a hurricane were to get too close to our city, and that they should all make

kits with their families that include water, food, flashlights, and first-aid items."
—*Lisa, preservice teacher, Tallahassee, Florida*

In reflecting on their service learning project, the kindergarten students demonstrated the wealth of knowledge they had gained and, more importantly, showed that they could readily empathize with others who are less fortunate.

"A lot of people's homes are gone because of Hurricane Katrina, so we all brought in money to send to them."
—*Kyle, age 4*

"I learned that hurricanes can ruin houses and buildings."
—*Amari, age 4*

"Hurricanes have strong winds that can blow down trees."
—*Susan, age 5*

"I made my mom and dad make a 'hurricane kit' in case a hurricane comes to our city."
—*Antonio, age 5*

"I learned that you can help people by giving money and making pictures because it will make people happy."
—*Jordan, age 5*

The voices of these children talking about their service learning project help us understand how much they can learn from such activities. Understanding how young children benefit from service learning becomes evident when we consider current theories about how children learn and develop. In turn, such understanding provides a rationale for the practice; it explains the "why" of service learning.

This chapter will demonstrate how service learning connects specifically to early childhood, and that it is much more than experiential learning or community service. Rather, it is a sound, research-based pedagogical approach that meets the developmental needs of young children and encourages character development.

The Benefits of Service Learning in Early Childhood Education

During the past 20 years, school reform efforts and the related emphasis on tougher standards and accountability have significantly influenced approaches to teaching and learning in classrooms in the United States. With No Child Left Behind, the pendulum has swung away from active, hands-on learning toward more traditional approaches in many areas of education. Faced with increasing pressures to improve test scores and provide more intensive early intervention, some teachers have had to adopt curriculum materials and pedagogical approaches that are more didactic. This shift has been especially difficult for early childhood teachers, in part because they recognize that the developmental needs of young learners are not always met through traditional instructional approaches. Service learning allows teachers to address the developmental needs of children while at the same time fulfilling high academic standards. Hence, through service learning, teachers can focus on helping their students perform basic skills at or above grade level, *without* abandoning strategies they know are good for young children.

The interdisciplinary and experiential natures of service learning are particularly appealing to early childhood educators. It is hardly surprising, therefore, that preschool, kindergarten, and primary grade teachers are adopting this approach. Service learning in early childhood education provides the following benefits for students and teachers as well as for the community:

- hands-on service
- hands-on experiential learning
- application of classroom activities to real-world issues
- projects that meet community needs
- learning that addresses curriculum standards and benchmarks
- real-world connections to the school curriculum
- curriculum enrichment
- experiences that combine learning with responsible citizenship

> Through service learning, teachers can focus on helping their students perform basic skills at or above grade level, *without* abandoning strategies they know are beneficial for young children.

Service Learning and Developmentally Appropriate Practice (DAP)

A specific appeal of service learning in early childhood education is that it is an approach that reflects principles outlined by the National Association for the Education of Young Children (NAEYC) in its publication, *Developmentally Appropriate Practice in Early Childhood Programs* (DAP). Drawing on the work of Jean Piaget, Lev Vygotsky, Erik Erikson, and others, this publication has had a major impact on the field of early childhood education. The DAP principles represent the consensus of opinion on current knowledge and thinking in the field.

According to its authors, DAP is a child-centered cognitive developmental approach to early childhood education. Such a perspective is based on the notion that children learn by actively constructing their own knowledge through interacting with materials, peers, and adults. A major goal of DAP is to make learning meaningful for the individual child, using practices that reflect both the child's age and individual needs. Strong emphasis is placed on learning to think critically, work cooperatively, and solve problems. Thus, in a developmentally appropriate classroom, the development of concepts and skills stressed through service learning is encouraged using investigations and hands-on activities. Teachers integrate the curriculum to reflect the interrelatedness of developmental domains by using strategies that include learning and activity centers, conceptual organizers, and thematic units. These strategies link together content from various subject areas and illustrate the connections that exist across disciplines.

According to DAP, the skills children will need as adults include the ability to:

- communicate well
- analyze situations and make reasonable judgments
- access information in a variety of ways
- continue to learn as they grow and the world changes

The DAP principles were published in response to the national trend toward more formal academic instruction for children instead of curricula designed for young children based on what is known *about* young children. One of the 12 principles explains that "children are active learners, drawing on direct physical and social experience as well as culturally transmitted knowledge to construct their understanding of the world around them."[1] In essence, by publishing the DAP principles, NAEYC challenged the field of early childhood education to adapt instructional approaches and curricula, while also making learning more meaningful and relevant to students.

Such challenges have not been restricted to the field of early childhood education. Higher education has also been called on to renew its historic commitment to service. Its foremost experts have urged colleges and universities to commit to the civic purposes of higher education and to engage their students in service learning and

> Traditional curriculum does not reflect current knowledge of human learning or brain development and fails to equip children with the higher-order thinking and problem-solving abilities needed in society today.

community-based learning.[2] At the same time, critiques of prevailing primary and secondary education curriculum content and methods have been addressed by such national organizations as the National Council of Teachers of Mathematics, the American Association for the Advancement of Science, the National Council of Teachers of English, the National Commission for the Social Studies, the National Association of Elementary School Principals, the Association for Supervision and Curriculum Development, and others. These reports reflect a growing consensus within the field of education that the traditional curriculum—with its emphasis on rote memorization, repetitive seatwork, teacher lecture, and drill and practice of isolated skills—does not reflect current knowledge of human learning or brain development and fails to equip children with the higher-order thinking and problem-solving abilities needed in society today. These national organizations call for schooling to place greater emphasis on:

- active, hands-on learning
- conceptual learning that leads to understanding and acquisition of basic skills
- meaningful, relevant learning experiences
- interactive teaching and cooperative learning
- a broad range of relevant content integrated across traditional subject matter divisions

Such tenets closely reflect the principles of service learning.

That said, the integration of service learning in early childhood education may perhaps be even more relevant and appealing than in other education levels, as the same fundamental concepts

[1] Copple & Bredekamp (2009), p. 13
[2] Brukardt et al. (2004)

developed during the early childhood years correspond with young children's understanding of their world. Moreover, an integrated approach permits teachers to design the curriculum in ways that meet the diversity in children's development and abilities.

An Overview of Theoretical Support for Service Learning with Young Children

The concepts of curricular integration and experiential learning are practically ubiquitous in early childhood education. The theories can be traced back to the ideas of John Dewey, William Heard Kilpatrick, Lev Vygotsky, and others. More recently, early childhood professionals have embraced approaches such as thematic teaching, the project approach, and experience-based learning. Yet, somewhat paradoxically, few attempts have been made to integrate service learning into early childhood education. Given that the approaches being embraced strive to make learning meaningful for the individual child, service learning projects and activities are a natural fit for the early childhood curriculum. This is because, in an early childhood classroom, the development of the learner and knowledge taught through service learning are encouraged by investigations and hands-on activities.

> Service learning projects and activities are a natural fit for the early childhood curriculum.

Theme-based instruction, or thematic integration, is particularly popular among early childhood educators today who want to make connections between multiple content areas. When using thematic integration, teachers often teach service learning concepts and skills without even realizing

it. Within the world of service learning, the term *content-specific integration* is used to describe the linking of a service learning concept with a curricular concept within the same lesson. Early childhood teachers who use a unit-based approach often use this form of integration. Content-specific integration offers opportunities for teachers to match objectives from service learning to content objectives and then plan appropriate learning activities, or vice versa.

In addition to integrated themes, teachers of young children have long recognized the importance of hands-on, experiential learning. Indeed, from the early beginnings of the kindergarten movement, components of a service learning pedagogy have been the staples of most approaches to early childhood education.

- Friedrich Fröebel, who developed the concept of kindergarten, claimed that "gifts and occupations," together with "gardening and nature study," were used to "develop the child according to his nature."[3]

- Maria Montessori, recognizing that children learn important concepts through their own activity, used "practical life exercises" to teach her students.[4]

- John Dewey and his colleague William Heard Kilpatrick also encouraged experiential learning by using projects and community-oriented themes. Although he did not call it service learning, Dewey recommended infusing kindergarten with "more natural, more direct, more real representations of current life."[5]

Today, service learning in early childhood holds true to the principles of teaching and learning developed long ago by the pioneers of our field. Indeed, interest in implementing service learning in school curricula stems all the way back to the work of early childhood pioneers, particularly Jean Piaget and Lev Vygotsky who introduced the theory of constructivist education. Constructivists believe that children learn through experience, interaction, and involvement in the world around them. Likewise, in service learning "young people are acknowledged, and see themselves as resourceful, knowledgeable, and agents of change who can

---

[3] Lilley, I. (1967)
[4] Montessori, M. (1912)
[5] Dewey, J. (1938)

harness their ideas, energy, and enthusiasm to benefit us all."[6] The phrase "benefit us all" is a foundation of both constructivism and service learning. It is the application of skills to the larger community that empowers children, and in turn builds character, morals, civic competency, and ethics.

Following on constructivist beliefs, an emerging body of research suggests that service learning can strengthen student learning in a number of important ways. When service learning is used in a structured manner with young children, it:

- allows teachers to apply academic, social, and personal skills to improve or supplement instruction.

- provides students with opportunities to make decisions that have real, versus hypothetical, results.

- enables participants to grow as individuals by encouraging them to work in cooperative groups. In doing so students gain respect for peers, increase their civic participation, and experience success regardless of their ability level.

- inspires students to gain a deeper understanding of themselves, their community, and society—an understanding that fosters the development of leaders who take initiative, solve problems, and work well in teams.[7]

Thus, as numerous past and present theories confirm, through service learning children can practice academic and social skills by integrating learning, exploring interests, building moral awareness and knowledge, learning the value of civic responsibility, developing a strong sense of character, learning to recognize a need, learning the values of voice and choice, and recognizing the need for collaboration and cooperation in school and the broader society. *Note:* A more in-depth discussion of early childhood theorists and service learning can be found in Chapter 13 on pages 164–168.

> Character education and service learning share many of the same goals.

Character Education and Service Learning

Among early childhood education initiatives, character education is at the forefront, with a renewed emphasis on bullying prevention and positive school climate. Not surprisingly, character education and service learning share many of the same goals. According to the Character Education Partnership, a nonprofit U.S. advocacy organization, character education encourages essential core and universal values such as respect, responsibility, citizenship, caring, and honesty throughout school. Understanding and practicing ethics and values can be accomplished through meaningful interactions in the community, and service learning offers students the opportunity to blend academic learning, universal values, and real-world applications into their daily lives.

Examples of the connection between character education and service learning can be found in numerous contexts across the United States. At the federal level, No Child Left Behind offers funding for character education programs. These programs include educating children about caring, citizenship, fairness, respect, and responsibility, which mirror the pillars of character according to Character Counts. In addition, the National and Community Service Trust Act (1993) defined service learning as the need to stress for active student involvement in the community to foster citizenship and responsibility, and also qualities of good character.

An example at the state level is the Pennsylvania Alliance for Character Education (PACE), an initiative of the Pennsylvania Service Learning Alliance that supports the integration of character education with service learning across Pennsylvania. This statewide effort employs service learning to build a bridge between character education and active, hands-on learning in the

---

[6] Kaye (2010), p. 2
[7] Bringle, Phillips, & Hudson (2004), Howard (2003)

community. Service learning programs in every state in the nation will likely continue to increase in the coming years with guidance and technical assistance from the Corporation for National and Community Service.

According to the Center for the 4th & 5th Rs—a program of the State University of New York at Cortland that promotes the development of moral and performance character in schools, families, and communities—there are seven reasons for providing character education.

1. It is the best way to make an enduring difference in the life of a student.

2. If done well, it improves academic achievement.

3. Many students are not getting strong character formation anywhere else.

4. It prepares students to respect others and live in a diverse society.

5. It gets to the root of a range of social/moral problems, including incivility, dishonesty, violence, premature sexual activity, and a poor work ethic.

6. It is the best preparation for the workplace.

7. Teaching the values of the culture is the work of civilization.[8]

These seven reasons are supported by research from past and present theorists in the field of character and moral education, such as John Dewey, Lawrence Kohlberg and Robert Selman, Thomas Lickona, Nel Noddings, and Maurice Elias, whose works are, in turn, closely tied to the tenets and benefits of service learning.

Service Learning Supports Differentiated Instruction

Most effective teachers routinely modify their instructional approaches to meet the diverse needs of their students. Such an approach whereby teachers provide learning opportunities for students of all abilities is commonly known as differentiated instruction. The flexible nature of service learning lends itself to this approach.

According to differentiation expert Carol Ann Tomlinson, differentiated instruction involves adjusting the content, process, and product of instruction so that *all* students learn, not just some students. This involves responding to learner differences such as readiness levels, learning styles, or interests. In organizing service learning, teachers can be proactive in planning various instructional activities that will facilitate learning in all students. For example, teachers can be flexible in their use of small learning groups in the classroom. During classroom-based service learning activities, teachers can vary the materials used by individuals or small groups, or they can allow children to produce different products. Similarly, pacing of the service learning activities can easily be modified in response to learner needs. Most important is the fact that service learning is a learner-centered approach whereby the instructional activities build on the prior knowledge that children bring to the task.

Service Learning and 21st Century Skills

A final compelling reason for using service learning with young children is that it allows teachers to address the knowledge and skills that students must master to succeed in work and life in the twenty-first century. According to the Partnership for 21st Century Skills, schools should integrate themes such as global awareness, civic literacy, and environmental literacy into academic core subjects.[9] While recognizing the importance of the traditional academic subjects, the Partnership also identifies student outcomes in the form of life and innovation skills. These skills include creative thinking, problem solving, reasoning, communication, and collaboration. Service learning can serve as a conduit through which such skills are developed.

Teaching a core of academic subjects is important in the primary grades. Service learning is an approach that allows teachers to effortlessly weave interdisciplinary themes into core academic subjects. Through service learning, skills such as critical thinking and communication can be enhanced *without* abandoning academic standards. Indeed, the service learning projects and activities highlighted in this book complement and enrich

---

[8] "7 Reasons for Character Education" at cortland.edu/character/
articles/7reasons.html.

[9] p21.org

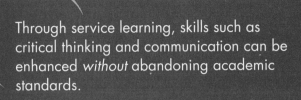

Through service learning, skills such as critical thinking and communication can be enhanced *without* abandoning academic standards.

traditional core subjects such as reading, mathematics, and social studies. In short, service learning creates an authentic context that allows teachers to integrate crucial skills into the teaching of core subjects.

Chapter Summary

There are many compelling reasons for using service learning as pedagogy with young children, because it's an approach that closely matches the way young children learn. It is also consistent with recommendations for best practices by professional associations, including the National Association for the Education of Young Children (NAEYC). These organizations highlight the importance of direct and meaningful experiences for young children; that is, the type of learning exemplified by service learning. Service learning allows teachers to design instruction for young children in developmentally appropriate ways. It is also an approach that supports differentiated instruction, while allowing teachers to design curricula using methods such as thematic or content integration. Possibly, the most compelling reason for using service learning in the early childhood classroom is that it can strengthen student learning. Beyond supporting the teaching of academic subjects, service learning also contributes toward broader school goals such as character education. Research shows that academic learning, social and moral development, civic skills, and character development are all supported when children engage in service learning projects.

Chapter 3

Service Learning and Early Childhood Academic Standards

In the previous chapter, you read about contributions of educational theorists and thinkers who provide strong support for service learning in the early childhood years. However, in the age of high-stakes testing, accountability, and No Child Left Behind, it is important that any educational endeavor also solidly meets content standards. Schools are required by law to demonstrate how each of their students makes "adequate yearly progress" in several key areas of the curriculum. In this chapter we demonstrate how service learning supports high academic standards across all content areas. In doing so, we confirm the ways in which service learning:

- matches how young children learn
- is developmentally appropriate
- makes learning meaningful for young children
- is not simply an "add on" program or activity
- provides children with real-world activities in a supportive context
- represents appropriate ways to teach academic content such as mathematics, reading, and writing
- guides students toward academic success

Put simply, service learning creates an environment that makes academic learning rich and relevant for young children.

Academic Standards and Best Practices

Service learning empowers students to become involved in their school and community, and to learn and grow through moral education. In addition to these outcomes, service learning projects help students successfully meet academic standards. Typically, academic standards specify what students should know and be able to do, how they might be asked to give evidence of standards, and how well they must perform. Standards assess content knowledge, performance, and proficiency. Most states have developed and adopted academic standards for each subject area. Recently, however, almost all states have adopted the Common Core State Standards for grades K–12 in English language arts and mathematics. In addition, several professional organizations provide national learning standards for their corresponding discipline areas. These organizations include:

- International Reading Association (IRA)
- National Council for Teachers of English (NCTE)
- National Council of Teachers of Mathematics (NCTM)
- National Council for the Social Studies (NCSS)
- National Science Education Standards (NSES)
- American Association for Health Education (AAHE)

18

- National Standards of Art Education (NSAE)
- International Society for Technology in Education (ISTE)

These diverse organizations share similar insights into learning and teaching. As discussed in *Best Practice: Today's Standards for Teaching and Learning in America's Schools,* these organizations agree on many recommendations, including:

- *less* whole-class, teacher-directed instruction
- *less* presentational, one-way transmission of information from teacher to student
- *less* classroom time devoted to fill-in-the-blank worksheets, workbooks, and other seatwork
- *less* rote memorization of facts and details
- *less* emphasis on competition and grades in school
- *less* use of and reliance on standardized tests
- *more* experiential, inductive, hands-on learning
- *more* active learning in the classroom, with all the attendant noise and movement of students doing, talking, and collaborating
- *more* emphasis on higher-order thinking, learning a field's key concepts and principles
- *more* deep study of a smaller number of topics, so that students internalize the field's methods of inquiry
- *more* reading of real texts: whole books, primary sources, and nonfiction materials
- *more* responsibility transferred to students for their work: goal setting, record keeping, monitoring, sharing, exhibiting, and evaluating
- *more* choice for students (such as, choosing their own books, writing topics, team partners, and research projects)
- *more* attention to effective needs and the varying cognitive styles of individual students
- *more* cooperative, collaborative activity, developing the classroom as an interdependent community

Clearly these best practices strongly resemble NAEYC's Developmentally Appropriate Practices (DAP) and many theories of experiential and constructivist learning. In fact, *Best Practice* highlights

13 related principles that characterize this model of education and mirror many of the goals of service learning projects. According to these principles, learning should be:

1. student-centered
2. experiential
3. holistic
4. authentic
5. expressive
6. reflective
7. social
8. collaborative
9. democratic
10. cognitive
11. developmental
12. constructivist
13. challenging

Service learning creates an environment that makes academic learning rich and relevant for young children.

The goal of service learning, much like *Best Practice,* is to develop these principles through community-based activities or projects that effectively meet state and national standards.

Service Learning Standards and Academic Success

The service learning standards outlined on pages 8–9 in Chapter 1 provide a well-defined set of common expectations for high quality practice. The standards are based on research from the field of service learning, expert opinion, and evidence from the larger literature of what works for student engagement and learning. These standards, when adhered to, will help ensure that service learning leads to academic success and student achievement.

The service learning standard for curriculum, for example, suggests that service learning experiences should be specifically designed to meet particular learning and curricular goals and/or content standards.

Taken together, the service learning standards and indicators can serve as a guide for effective practice and positive outcomes. In order to understand how service learning projects can effectively meet academic standards, it is important to discuss each subject area individually, with examples of specific projects that meet specific goals. In this chapter the subject areas are divided into language arts, mathematics, science, social studies, fine arts, technology, and health.

Language Arts Standards

Beginning with language arts, the IRA and the NCTE have selected many standards regarding the goals of teaching language lessons to young children. Similarly, the Common Core State Standards for English language arts define what students should know and be able to do. The IRA/NCTE standards ensure that students are able to:

- read a wide range of print/literature from many periods and for many purposes
- apply a wide range of strategies to comprehend, interpret, and evaluate
- adjust the use of spoken, written, and visual language
- employ a wide range of strategies as they write
- apply knowledge of language structure and conventions

Language Arts Project Spotlight:
Postcards for the Rainforests

As a service learning project, students in a first-grade class in Tallahassee, Florida, studying the Amazon Rainforest chose to learn about the topic and write postcards to the governor of their state asking that he help preserve the rainforests. The students read stories from a variety of books, magazines, encyclopedias, newspapers, and websites. They collectively joined in many discussions about the importance of the rainforests, what resources rainforests produce, and how they are being cut down every day.

Next, the students worked with a variety of materials to create individual postcards for their state's governor. These postcards acted as student reflections on the issue. Students wrote to the governor with their priorities in mind and hoped to make a difference. Some postcards were a personal greeting to the governor recommending changes for the future, some were full of facts and information about rainforests, and others were photos of beautiful rainforests that will be missed if the destruction continues. Each child personalized the assignment to mean something different. Some hoped to inform, others chose to show their concern, and some just wished to be heard.

Students further extended the relevance of the assignment by working through the writing process: selecting, prewriting, drafting, revising, and editing. Each student's postcard was an ideal representation of that student's writing skills, personal opinion, and agenda regarding the care of the world's rainforests—which were the goals of the assignment. These goals closely mirror the Common Core State Standards as well as national standards developed by the NCTE and IRA, making this service learning project a clear example of how academic learning can take place through community learning, social interactions, and active hands-on involvement.

- conduct research on issues and interests by generating ideas and questions
- use a variety of resources

Lastly, these organizations stress that "students participate as knowledgeable, reflective, creative, and critical members of a variety of literacy communities, and that students use spoken, written, and visual language to accomplish their own purposes."[1] With a standard like "accomplish their own purposes," it is no wonder that service learning projects—which focus on empowerment, moral education, reflection, and experiential learning—meet this goal. Students are submerged in the learning process as they learn through experience. They then reflect upon those experiences, and in turn, gain new knowledge.

Mathematics Standards

Service learning projects can also help students meet math standards. *Best Practice* suggests that lessons aimed at teaching math skills should:

- increase the use of mathematics as communication through discussions, reading, writing, and listening
- provide everyday problems from which to draw logical conclusions
- encourage children to make mathematical connections and find solutions through active involvement and/or cooperative group work

In addition, both *Best Practice* and the NCTM suggest that lessons should:

- connect mathematics to other subjects and to the real world
- develop number sense
- develop spatial sense
- teach collection and organization of data
- teach pattern recognition
- develop the use of tables and graphs

The Common Core State Standards for mathematics, while describing content standards, also describe standards for mathematical practice. These standards include the following goals. Students should:

- make sense of problems and persevere in solving them
- model with mathematics
- use appropriate tools strategically
- reason abstractly and quantitatively

Guided by math standards, teachers are encouraged in *Best Practice* to connect the practices to the content in math instruction and to teach for understanding. Practices in the early grades should help students engage with math by providing opportunities for children to represent problems coherently, justify conclusions, and apply mathematics to practical situations.

Mathematics Project Spotlight:
Helping Hands for Pensacola

A school-wide service learning project conducted in Tallahassee, Florida, titled "Helping Hands for Pensacola," involved the entire community as students, teachers, and families collected pennies for a hurricane relief fund dedicated to Pensacola. The students demonstrated several Common Core State Standards and NCTM standards, such as number and spatial sense, by counting the pennies and spreading them out onto traced "helping hands" hand prints. This lesson also showed students' ability to organize and collect materials—students made piles of five and ten pennies to alleviate confusion in the counting process. This plan intertwined problem-solving skills in both math and science, as students tested hypotheses before finding the most effective strategy for counting the pennies.

---

[1] Zemelman, Daniels, & Hyde (1998), p. 30

Science Standards

While meeting national standards for reading and writing, students involved in the rainforest project (page 20) were also successful at meeting science standards. The components of the rainforest: the trees, animals, and weather, were all discussed throughout the lesson. Students began to understand how living things interact with their environment, specifically the consequences of using limited natural resources, thereby meeting the national science standard: Standard C: Life Science: the characteristics of organisms, life cycles of organisms, organisms and the environment.

As found in *Best Practice* and the National Science Education Standards (NSES), many recommendations for teaching science resemble components of a service learning project. Students are to be involved in hands-on activities that include:

- observation
- reflection
- application
- hypotheses
- questioning
- problem solving
- in-depth study of thematic topics

These standards and the organization that recommends them discourage science from being segregated from students' lives and other areas of the curriculum. Science is not to be limited to textbooks and vocabulary. Students should experience learning through active involvement in an activity that can teach many areas of the curriculum.

The national science standards most commonly met through service learning are those in the category of life science. Examples of service learning projects meeting these standards are discussed in the following sections, followed by projects that meet other national science standards.

Note: Many of the project examples listed in this chapter are described in more depth in Part Three.

Project Examples: Life Science

- In the previously discussed "Postcards for the Rainforest" project (page 20), students learned about the different animals and plants that live in the rainforest and how they coexist.

- A classroom and school recycling effort focused on the use of limited natural resources (see Chapter 12).

- A project advocating for endangered species (elephants, sea turtles, etc.) required students to explain how changes in an environment influences whether an animal can live and reproduce (see Chapter 12).

- In the project "Growing Flowers for Others," students planted flowers to take to hospital patients (see Chapter 10).

- A kindergarten class planted a small garden outside their classroom in an attempt to attract butterflies and help beautify the school (see Chapter 10).

- A first-grade class planted a miniature rainforest in their classroom to help explain the importance of the rainforest. The students were responsible for watering the plants and ensuring their successful growth.

All of these projects enabled students to successfully meet objectives in life science. They became aware of the basic needs of plants (air, water, light, and soil), could identify the parts of a plant, and were able to witness the life cycle of plants.

Project Examples: Personal and Social Perspectives on Science

The Personal and Social Perspectives category of the NSES includes understanding changes in environments and different types of resources. Examples include:

- "Postcards for the Rainforest" required students to study resources such as medicines that the rainforest fosters, as well as how the changing environment (clear-cutting, pollution, etc.) affects the organisms that live there.

- A recycling or school cleanup project clearly establishes this connection (see Chapter 12).

- A project that focuses on the threat that pollution poses to marine life also meets these standards (see Chapter 12).

Project Examples: Earth and Climate Science

- To meet national standards in the Earth and Climate Science category, one class discussed weather patterns including temperature, wind, and precipitation. The students were able to explain how pollution causes acid rain, a harmful type of precipitation. In addition to learning about pollution, they were able to make a connection between the causes of pollution (including too much garbage) and the weather (see Chapter 12).

- Another project provided aid to hurricane victims. The class discussed the causes and characteristics of hurricanes and the influences that such natural disasters have on communities. After learning about the destruction caused by the powerful storm, the students were compelled to help the victims with money, food, clothing, books, and school supplies (see Chapter 11).

Project Examples: Sharing Science Information with Others

Some service learning projects involved writing letters or cards to others sharing information that students recently learned in science class.

- A kindergarten class chose to create and distribute spring cards to those who are terminally ill and in hospice care. While drawing pictures of flowers on the cards, the students studied plants, seeds, and flowers. Identifying the different parts of flowers and recognizing how flowers develop from seeds is a NSES learning objective under Life Cycles of Organisms (see Chapter 9).

- Another class wrote letters to troops stationed overseas. The students expressed how much they missed and wanted the soldiers to come home, and also tried to brighten their day by relaying some fascinating facts about the planets and solar system (see Chapter 9).

Therefore, while students learned about flowers or space, they also developed a sense of compassion and pride for being able to make someone's day a little better with a beautiful card.

Social Studies Standards

Best Practice offers many suggestions for social studies lessons that mirror the elements of a service learning project. There is great emphasis on activities that engage students in inquiry and problem solving related to significant human issues. *Best Practice* also promotes student decision making and participation in wider social, political, and economic affairs, so they share a sense of civic responsibility for the welfare of their school and

Social Studies Project Spotlight:
Letters to Troops

In the "Letters to Soldiers" project (page 121), students learned about world issues, geography, and civic responsibility as they wrote to troops at war overseas. In corresponding with individuals in distant regions, they gained a broader sense of community. The students also developed senses of honor and duty by commending the soldiers for their sacrifices on behalf of the nation. Furthermore, while meeting specific national social studies standards, such as Theme #10: Civic Ideals and Practices and Theme #4: Individual Development Groups and Identity, students accomplished language arts goals by writing letters. This is yet another example of how service learning can reach across the curriculum for academic learning, while promoting character education and empowerment (see Chapter 9).

community. In addition, the guide recommends that students develop understanding in areas of history, economics, sociology, geography, political science, and psychology. They should examine all cultures represented in a community, and their understanding of social studies should extend to other areas of the curriculum as well.

Once again, overlapping curricular areas is a strategy that is effectively applied through service learning. The National Council for the Social Studies (NCSS) divides social studies into five areas: civics, economics, geography, U.S. history, and world history. These areas are represented in nearly every service learning project, since such projects typically involve serving the community, helping others, and learning the role of a citizen in democracy. Recently, the NCSS updated their standards document by providing a set of principles by which social studies content can be selected. These principles are described in 10 themes or categories that represent a way of organizing knowledge about human experience in the world. These 10 themes include culture; time; continuity and change; and people, places, and environments. Complementing the 10 themes are learning expectations for students at different grade levels.

Fine Arts Standards

It is very common for early childhood lessons to incorporate an art activity. Young children are still growing and developing understandings of themselves and their abilities. Many teachers find it effective to use art as a form of reflection on information taught in a lesson. *Best Practice* suggests that you increase students' originality, choice, and responsibility in art making. It recommends using art as an element of talent development by increasing the number and duration of art projects. Fine arts projects include theater, visual art, music, and dance, which allow children to be creative and expressive and learn more about their physical and cognitive abilities.

Service learning projects can incorporate many of the fine arts, especially visual art. In fact, the National Standards of Art Education (NSAE) asks that students make connections between visual arts and the real world. Visual art is often used in

the reflection stage of service learning, along with theater, music, or dance. Projects that involve art often focus on teaching another aspect of the curriculum, such as social studies, language arts, science, or math. For example, in one project, students worked to save sea animals and designed posters and pictures to hang in the school hallways, using visual art as a means of advocacy. In addition to meeting other content standards, these artworks demonstrated the children's knowledge of the proper uses of art materials and the information that can be conveyed through art, and enabled each student to artistically display his or her understanding of the service learning project. Different students may take away different information from a service learning project, and art is an effective way to recognize each child's appreciation of the project.

Project Examples: Fine Arts

- One class chose to recycle used paper in their classroom after learning about the harmful effects that too much garbage has on the environment. Each student drew a picture on recycled paper illustrating their understanding of recycling and its benefits. The class then learned about the concept of a *collage* when they decorated a plastic recycling bin with all the students' drawings. Because the students learned about and used a new art technique, this project met a national visual arts standard: Content Standard #1: Understanding and applying media, techniques, and processes (see Chapter 12).

- Some classes involved in cleaning up trash around the school or advocating for endangered species had student representatives discuss their project on the school morning news show or talk to other classes. This demonstration of the projects met national theater standards. For young children, talking in front of even a small crowd requires much preparation. They need to practice not only *what* they will say, but their composure as well. They learn to adjust the volume and tempo of their speech when speaking to a group. Some children found it helpful to write a script and memorize it, rather than improvising (see Chapter 12).

- Teachers have also readily incorporated music and dance into service learning. A class can learn and practice a song (with or without instruments) or a dance to perform for residents of a nursing home, providing the residents with stimulation and exercise. Or a class that is advocating to save an animal species could make up a song to help teach others (families, friends, other classes, etc.) about what threatens these animals.

Technology Standards

To meet the National Educational Technology Standards (NETS), you can use software, online applications, websites, or other technology components that relate to the service learning project. For instance, the students involved in "Postcards for the Rainforest" (page 20) could have worked with a computer program or app that teaches about animals of the rainforest and asks students to write stories or practice math skills. Even young students can use technology during projects to make PowerPoint presentations or design online public service announcements on topics of interest.

During service learning, students use technology to accomplish numerous goals, such as:

- perform academic tasks
- solve community problems and needs
- collaborate with peers, experts, and others to contribute to a content-related knowledge base
- compile, synthesize, produce, and distribute information, models, and other creative works
- use the keyboard, mouse, and other common input and output devices (including adaptive devices when necessary) efficiently and effectively
- use technology tools and resources for managing and communicating information
- use online information resources for collaboration, research, and publication

Health Standards

A service learning project could be just as effective at meeting national health standards as a classroom lesson on good health. The American Association for Health Education (AAHE) identifies the need

Health Project Spotlights:
Postcards for the Rainforest

As an example of a service learning project that meets health standards, we once again revisit "Postcards for the Rainforest" (see page 20). For this project, the children wrote letters, designed pictures, and ultimately shared a goal of saving the world's rainforest. In doing so, they learned about diverse animals, plants, resources, and medicines from these rainforests. Then, the students set a goal to convince their governor that destroying our rainforests will threaten our good health and clean air.

Letters to Patients

Another project involved students writing letters to patients in a children's hospital. The students were able to identify diseases and other health-related problems faced by children. They discussed how the children they were writing to were in poor health. Through their service learning project, the students understood that the children in the hospital were not as fortunate as them and were able to offer some comfort to those children (see Chapter 9).

for young children to understand the concepts related to:

- good health and disease prevention

- how to avoid health risks

- how to use effective interpersonal communication skills that enhance health

- how to use goal setting and decision making to increase health

- how to advocate for personal, family, and community health

Chapter Summary

The successful approaches outlined by *Best Practice* and national organizations as a means to achieve high academic standards can all be captured through service learning projects. By adopting service learning, you can use instructional strategies that all of the professional organizations consider to be exemplary practices. Service learning is an approach that supports children's learning across all areas of the curriculum, including language arts, mathematics, social studies, science, fine arts, technology, and health. Examples from tried-and-tested projects, such as those in Part Three of this book, clearly demonstrate children's learning through service.

Chapter 4

How to Design Service Learning with Young Children

This chapter will outline an assortment of ideas for engaging in service learning in early childhood, no matter if you are at a novice, an intermediate, or an advanced level of expertise with the practice. Maybe you are just one step ahead of your students; if so, we will provide clear scaffolding to help guide you through your first service learning experience. Once you become more comfortable with the language, project integration, and forms, you'll start branching out on your own and using the ideas and pieces that make the most sense to you. If you are a veteran of service learning, you may find new ideas here and ways to extend your current practices with young children.

When designing projects, it is helpful to think of service learning as an *evolutionary* (versus revolutionary) process. In many cases, you can make just a few tweaks to what you are already doing and add a service learning element. This is much easier and more realistic than scrapping what you have been doing for years and trying to replace it with something altogether different. Also, focus on an idea that is personally (as well as professionally) interesting to you. You will enjoy the effort more if the service learning is relevant to you. The following sections give recommendations for project design for teachers at all levels of service learning knowledge and experience.

Service Learning Level: Novice

Novice-Level Thinking: Help! I've never done this before, but it sounds like a good idea.

1. Prepare and plan your service learning lesson using one of the following two options.

   Option A: Use the Service Learning Lesson Plans in This Book

   Review the sample lesson plans in Part 3 (pages 117–161). Match one of the lessons to your classroom needs by choosing a lesson that:

   - complements your upcoming curriculum
   - would be interesting to your students
   - focuses on a skill your students need
   - addresses a need in your community

   Once you've chosen a lesson, use the **Service Learning Lesson Plan** (pages 63–64) to tailor it to your class.

   - Is your need the same as the one stated in the sample lesson plan? If not, modify the plan. Do the same for the purpose and the participants.
   - Be sure to specify both a curricular outcome and a social outcome.

○ Your evaluation will include an assessment of the objectives and the purpose of the service learning project. Remember, you want students to reflect on, share, and celebrate what they have learned with others.

○ Check to see that you have the materials needed for the lesson. There are resources listed on pages 205–207 that support the sample lessons.

○ When filling out the "Participants" section, you may want to use forms elsewhere in this book to guide you. For example, if you have several community helpers, you can use the **Community Contacts** tool on pages 59–60.

○ If you find you need more lesson structure, you might also want to use the **General Lesson Plan for Service Learning** on pages 65–66.

Option B: Use Your Own Curriculum

Examine your curriculum. What area lends itself to a service learning project?

○ In which part of your curriculum do you already have students working in pairs or groups? Is this a hands-on area, such as art, dramatic play, music, math, or science? If so, think about a service learning project that fits into one of those curriculum areas.

○ Is there a holiday coming up that you want to target? Does your class have a favorite book that lends itself to a service project?

○ If you are using active learning as an everyday instructional strategy, you may want to choose two different ideas—a holiday focus and a favorite book, for instance—and let your class vote on which one they'd like to pursue.

○ If you are new to managing active learning experiences, or are in a school that has limited support for service learning, you may decide to choose the service learning topic yourself the first time and plan

your student work groups. *Remember:* this is meant to be an enjoyable learning experience; your first time should not be your last time! So if you need a little more control over the situation—take it.

2. Once you know what your service learning focus will be, the following forms from this book will be helpful. You can use these in any order, and not every blank has to be filled in right now. At this stage, you are getting yourself mentally ready for the project and beginning to gather physical resources.

○ **Curriculum Connections** (pages 50–51 or 54–55)

○ **Ready, Set, Serve!** (pages 69–70)

○ **Teacher Expectations** (pages 71–72)

○ **Student Artifact Release Form** (page 40)

○ **Student Photo Release Form** (page 41)

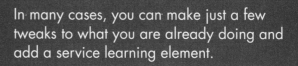

In many cases, you can make just a few tweaks to what you are already doing and add a service learning element.

3. Now that you are prepared, it is time to introduce the project. Unless your class has already voted on the service learning project, this is when you will tell them about it. Here are some forms and resources to help you do this:

○ **Preparing Students for Service Learning** (page 48) provides a list of ways to introduce your class to service learning.

○ **Brainstorming the Activity** (pages 42–43)

○ **Beginning to Serve** (pages 44–45)

○ *26 Big Things Small Hands Do* (Free Spirit Publishing, 2008) and *The Giving Book* (Watering Can, 2005) are two great children's books you can use to introduce service learning.

4. At this point, your students have provided you with a lot of input on what they think about the service learning project. Now, determine if these forms are needed for your project:

     ○ **Community Contacts** (see pages 59–60)

     ○ **Service Learning Project Overview** (see pages 61–62)

5. You also need to decide on one or several reflection ideas to use throughout the service learning experience. Some choices include:

     ○ **Service Learning Reflection Activity** (see pages 84–85)

     ○ **Service Learning KWL Chart** (see page 88)

     ○ **Service Learning KFL Chart** (see page 89)

     ○ **Service Learning Postcard Reflection** (see page 90)

     ○ **Service Learning Friendly Letter Planning Form** (see page 91)

     ○ **Service Learning ABC Reflection** (see page 93)

     ○ **Service Learning Log** (see pages 95–96)

     ○ **Service Learning Chain of Events** (see page 97)

     ○ **Service Learning Hand Chart** (see page 99)

     ○ **Service Learning Spider Chart** (see page 100)

6. It is now time to write your lesson plan. For the first few times planning a service learning project, you might use the following formats:

     ○ **Service Learning Lesson Plan** (pages 63–64)

     ○ **Curricular Skills Checklist** (page 58). This form ensures that your lesson plan is written and your objectives are clearly stated. If you want to use this form, your lesson objectives—which can now be broken down into skills if they are not already—can be easily transferred over to this tool.

     ○ Also, review your **Brainstorming the Activity** and **Teacher Expectations** forms. Can you fill in anything else? In addition, it is now time to contact all your resource people—parent helpers, community helpers, etc.

7. Follow your lesson plan and begin your service learning project. It might only take one day or it might take several days. Keep close tabs on your academic and social objectives. If your project takes more than one day, plan a reflection activity at the end of each day and review the previous day's learning.

8. Evaluate the service learning experience. Use one of the following forms:

     ○ **Child-to-Child Evaluation of Service Learning** (see pages 104–105)

     ○ **Service Learning Smiley Evaluation** (see page 106)

     ○ **Service Learning Portrait Assessment** (see page 108)

     ○ **Service Learning TOW Assessment** (see pages 109–110)

     ○ **Teacher Assessment of the Service Learning Project** (see pages 113–114)

     ○ **Teacher Assessment of the Service Learning Site or Partner Organization** (see page 115)

9. Do not forget to celebrate your service learning experience and document your learning for others. Use the tool **Documentation Ideas** (page 102).

10. Remember to file your **Curricular Skills Checklist** (page 58) in your portfolio or grade book so you will have that information when you need to report to parents and on report cards and progress reports.

Service Learning Level: Intermediate

Intermediate-Level Thinking: I think I am getting the hang of service learning. I have the basics down, but there are still some areas that I need to develop further.

1. Look at the sample lesson plans in Part 3 (pages 117–161) to get an idea of the variety of topics available. Choose a lesson that:

   ○ complements your upcoming curriculum

   ○ would be interesting to your students

   ○ focuses on a skill your students need

   ○ addresses a need in your community

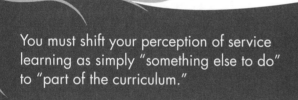

You must shift your perception of service learning as simply "something else to do" to "part of the curriculum."

2. Based on your past experiences with service learning, ask yourself:

   ○ Do I want to develop more detailed plans and work more on curricular connections?

   ○ Do I need to outreach more to parents, teachers, and community resources?

   ○ Has reflection been difficult to implement?

   ○ When it came to documenting and demonstrating their previous service learning projects, have my students told enough people?

   ○ Do I need celebration ideas?

Service learning should be integrated into your classroom; this is a gradual process. You know the basics, and now we want to help you bite off one more piece and develop it further before moving to the next piece. So, find the "topic for improvement" from the following that matches the area you want to develop further and get to it!

Topic for Improvement: Planning and Curricular Connections

Do you see your service learning lessons as add-on lessons? If your answer is yes, then in addition to working on planning and curricular connections, you must also shift your perception of service learning as simply "something else to do" to "part of the curriculum." This perception shift is the biggest hurdle faced by classroom teachers. As you make that shift, consider the following strategies.

- **More Focused Planning.** The service learning lesson examples in Part Three do not use traditional lesson plan formats. If you'd like more help and structure with planning, take the examples and transfer the information to a more traditional lesson plan format (see the **General Lesson Plan for Service Learning** on pages 65–66). Using a more familiar lesson plan format will help you see the standards and objectives taught and assessed through the service learning project, thus helping you to start thinking of it as part of the curriculum. Evaluate the learning using the **Curricular Skills Checklist** (page 58) and then record the information in your grade book or portfolios.

- **Integrating Service Learning Goals in Class.** Look at the **Curriculum Connections** tools (pages 50–51 and 54–55). In the middle box, write the service learning need, purpose, and outcomes (social and academic). Several things can happen at this point:

   ○ The service learning becomes the curricular theme for the classroom.

   ○ The service learning supplements the existing theme or curriculum of the classroom in all or some of the areas.

   ○ The service learning replaces some of the existing curriculum, e.g., a project on saving elephants might replace the existing science curriculum on animals, not supplement it, while you would plan the added math and literacy components.

Topic for Improvement: Making Connections to Parents, Teachers, and Community Partners

If outreach is where you would like to make improvements, first ask yourself these questions:

In my past service learning projects, who has been involved and how were they involved? What areas of service learning are working well and what areas need help?

Who do I know who would be willing to help?

Who might know something about my project and would make sense for me to contact?

Next, follow these tips.

- **Make a list of contacts.** Include parents, teachers, or community members who you could call on to begin to develop service learning relationships. Just choose two or three to start. Perhaps begin by adding more parents on a service learning project. Reflect on the impact of the parents on the students and the project, and then make adjustments accordingly. In the next project, work with the parents to add more community members, and then make more adjustments as needed. When you are ready, begin to involve more teachers in service learning.

- **Take it slowly.** You might spend the whole year just adding more parents and finding different ways to involve them. Keep track of this information using the **Community Contacts** form (pages 59–60), amending it slightly to include parents. At the beginning-of-the-year open house, talk to the parents about the class's focus on service learning and ask them how they are involved in the community. Your students may want to become involved in some of the same projects and activities as their parents.

- **Find out what community members know about young children.** Many community members need a little training when talking to or working with young children for the first time, so be prepared to ask and answer some questions. You might provide them with a list of helpful hints or conduct a brief training session.

- **Thank everyone for their time and help.** This may seem like a no-brainer, but it is easy to overlook if you have a busy schedule. As the teacher, you might want to plan this in as part of your reflection, documentation, or celebration stages and involve your students. Having students write thank-you notes expands their service learning.

Topic for Improvement: Implementing Reflection

We often get so focused on the actual *doing* of the service learning that reflection is just tacked on to the end of the project instead of being integrated throughout. If this sounds familiar, you are in good company! To enrich reflection, you'll want to implement ongoing reflection strategies that take longer and may continue over multiple days. These tools are a great place to start:

- **Service Learning ABC Reflection** (page 93)
- **Service Learning Log** (pages 95–96)
- **Service Learning Chain of Events** (page 97)
- **Service Learning Hand Chart** (page 99)
- **Service Learning Spider Chart** (page 100)

Topic for Improvement: Making Documentation Work

Spreading the word about service learning and describing your specific service learning project goals is what documentation is all about. Remember to stress what the community need was and how the service learning project addressed that need. What structures already exist in your school that you can tap in to—morning announcements, newsletters, websites, student councils, PTA or PTSA groups, or other organizations? Use these established structures first, then branch out and try some of the other suggestions on **Documentation Ideas** (page 102).

1

Service Learning Level: Advanced

Advanced-Level Thinking: I understand the pedagogy and methodology of service learning and have been successful in implementing it in my classroom. Now I'd like to extend my practice and get other teachers involved, mentor a novice teacher, start a student service learning group, and/or make service learning a school-wide focus.

Extension: Involving Other Teachers in Service Learning

If you know teachers in your school who are interested in learning more about service learning, here are some ideas to increase their knowledge and get them excited about the practice.

- **Start a book club.** Many schools want or even require teachers to be involved in professional development, and book clubs are a great way to meet the individual needs and professional goals of teachers.* In the fall, read the book, learn the content, and choose a project. In the spring, the book club switches to a service learning action group. The teachers in the group can plan one service learning project to work on together, or each teacher can implement his or her own project and use the group for support and ideas. The group can also be a combination of the two, with some teachers working together and others doing their own thing. Some book suggestions are:

    - *The Complete Guide to Service Learning: Proven, Practical Ways to Engage Students in Civic Responsibility, Academic Curriculum, and Social Action* by Cathryn Berger Kaye (Free Spirit Publishing, 2010)

    - *The New 50 Simple Things Kids Can Do to Save the Earth* by Earthworks Group (Andrews McMeel Publishing, 2009)

- **Invite teachers to participate.** As your class plans for a service learning project, reach out to interested teachers and involve them in some fun and low-responsibility aspect of

the project. After they have participated and witnessed the impact that service learning can have on students and the community, they might be more willing to co-plan with you on the next project or be mentored by you on a project of their own.

Extension: Mentoring a Novice Teacher in Service Learning

If you know a teacher who wants to learn more about service learning, help him or her as a mentor or coach. Follow these steps:

1. Find out why he or she is interested in service learning. Is there a specific cause that has inspired this teacher to want to engage in service learning or is the interest for broader reasons? Knowing this information will help you tailor your mentoring to meet the teacher's needs.

2. Schedule regular times to meet. Plan to meet in both of your classrooms or meet outside of school at happy hour, over dinner, or at a community event or location that might be a possible service learning site or partner.

3. Put forms to use. Once you know whether you will be working on the same service learning project or two different projects, use the following forms. As a mentor, these forms provide you with valuable thinking and processing skills that will aide in communication between you and your protégé. You can use these in any order, and not every space has to be filled out right now. The goal is to get both of you mentally ready and beginning to pull together the physical resources.

    - **Curriculum Connections** (pages 50–51 or 54–55)
    - **Ready, Set, Serve!** (pages 69–70)
    - **Teacher Expectations** (pages 71–72)
    - **Student Artifact Release Form** (page 40)
    - **Student Photo Release Form** (page 41)

---

*See Chapter 14, pages 169–201, for more information about service learning and professional development.

4. Now that you are both prepared, it is time to act. If the novice teacher's class has not voted on the service learning project, then now is when she or he will introduce the project to the class. Below are ideas for how to do this:

   o **Preparing Students for Service Learning** (page 48) provides a list of ways to introduce service learning

   o **Brainstorming the Activity** (pages 42–43)

   o **Beginning to Serve** (pages 44–45)

   o A great children's book that we use to introduce service learning is *26 Big Things Small Hands Do* (Free Spirit Publishing, 2008)

5. The students have provided both of you with lots of input about what their views are regarding the service learning projects. Now is time to add to the brainstorming and expectations forms and consider if the following forms are needed:

   o **Community Contacts** (pages 59–60)

   o **Service Learning Project Overview** (pages 61–62)

6. You both also need to decide on one or several reflection ideas to use throughout the service learning experience. Some choices include:

   o **Service Learning Reflection Activity** (see pages 84–85)

   o **Service Learning KWL Chart** (see page 88)

   o **Service Learning KFL Chart** (see page 89)

   o **Service Learning Postcard Reflection** (see page 90)

   o **Service Learning Friendly Letter Planning Form** (see page 91)

   o **Service Learning ABC Reflection** (see page 93)

   o **Service Learning Log** (see pages 95–96)

   o **Service Learning Chain of Events** (see page 97)

   o **Service Learning Hand Chart** (see page 99)

   o **Service Learning Spider Chart** (see page 100)

7. It is now time to write the lesson plans. For the first few times modeling how to plan a service learning project, we suggest the following:

   o **Service Learning Lesson Plan** (pages 63–64)

   o **Curricular Skills Checklist** (page 58)— once the lesson plan is written and your objectives are clearly stated, your objectives—which can now be broken down into skills if they are not already— can be easily transferred over to this tool

8. Review your **Brainstorming the Activity** and **Teacher Expectations** forms again. Can you fill in anything else? Also, it is now time to contact all of your individual resource people— parent helpers, community helpers, etc.

9. Follow your individual lesson plans and begin your service learning project. It might only take one day or it might take several days. Keep close tabs on your academic and social objectives. If your project takes more than one day, plan a reflection activity at the end of each day and review the previous day's learning.

10. Evaluate the service learning experience. You can use:

    o **Child-to-Child Evaluation of Service Learning** (see pages 104–105)

    o **Service Learning Smiley Evaluation** (see page 106)

    o **Service Learning Portrait Assessment** (see page 108)

    o **Service Learning TOW Assessment** (see pages 109–110)

    o **Teacher Assessment of the Service Learning Project** (see pages 113–114)

    o **Teacher Assessment of the Service Learning Site or Partner Organization** (see page 115)

11. Do not forget to celebrate the service learning experience and document or share your learning with each other. Several documentation ideas are listed on **Documentation Ideas** (page 102).

12. Remember to file your **Curricular Skills Checklist** (page 58) in your portfolio or grade book so you will have that information when you need it.

When you have finished, reflect on the service learning process with the novice teacher. What does he or she want to change or do differently the next time? Acknowledge his or her progress and willingness to try this innovative teaching strategy. Then, encourage the teacher you've mentored to begin thinking about his or her next service learning project!

Extension: Starting a Student-Oriented Service Learning Group

As an advanced service learning teacher, you are probably integrating service learning into several areas of the curriculum. The simplest way to organize a service learning group in your school is to plan and implement projects with your own classes, and then invite interested students to participate. The process may look like one of these options:

Option A: School-Day Service Learning Group

1. Choose a class service learning project that has a school-wide focus, such as beautification, cleanup, recycling, playground safety, etc.

2. Have students announce their efforts to the school and invite interested participants to join them in a before- or after-school meeting, or during lunch. Send home family permission forms.

3. Organize the different work groups needed for the service learning project, for which students can sign up. Each work group, led by the students, meets for about 20 minutes once a week, usually at the beginning or end of the school day, until the service learning project is completed.

4. Provide reflections for each group along the way.

5. At the end of the project, facilitate group reflection, evaluation, and documentation.

The benefits of running this type of service learning group are:

- There are minimal after-school hours.
- Different students can participate each time depending on the project.
- The school community benefits, so the school advisory committee (SAC) or PTA/PTSA would make a good financial alliance.
- Your classroom continues to do service learning as it always has, you are just allowing others to participate with you.

Some drawbacks of this type of group are:

- Meeting with the different groups during the school day will take away from some of your instructional time.
- Most service learning projects are school- or campus-based.
- The project may not be curriculum-based service learning.

Option B: After-School Service Learning Group

1. Send out notices to students and parents that a new group will be starting; include the mission and meeting times. Provide a space at the bottom of the form for the family's and student's signatures.

2. Hold an orientation meeting. Elect or choose officers for the group, or else choose leaders for each project. Vote on projects, form smaller groups, and divide up the tasks to be accomplished for the next meeting.

3. Before the next meeting, students should check in with the sponsor at a designated time so the sponsor can report on the group's progress and make suggestions for the next steps.

4. Make the first projects relatively simple and easy to complete. This is important so that students do not lose interest in the group and so they can follow the process from planning to documentation without too much time in between.

5. As the year progresses and the service learning group becomes more entrenched in the school, the projects can become more involved, complex, and ongoing.

The benefits of running this type of service learning group are:

- It can really work to achieve the school mission and achieve community outreach.

- All grades can participate.

- The school community benefits, so the SAC or PTA/PTSA would make a good financial alliance.

Some drawbacks of this type of group are:

- Most service learning projects are school- or campus-based.

- The project may not be curriculum-based service learning.

Extension: Developing a School-Wide Service Learning Focus

If you want service learning to become a school-wide focus, you need the support of your administration. If your administrators are only lukewarm, it is probably not a good idea to try to move forward with this idea until you have their buy-in. A school-wide effort is a huge amount of work, and your administrators need to be on board 100 percent for it to have a chance of working. Once the administrators are on board, teachers' buy-in is also needed. Most schools form a Service Learning Committee (SLC) that works together for at least

School Spotlight:
Elementary School, Northern California

One elementary school formed a truly united service learning focus. It started out with several classes creating small gardens and growing food for the local food bank and homeless shelter. Many more students wanted to help, so more teachers became involved the next year. During the second year, the homeless shelter administrators brought some of its residents to the school to help tend the gardens and work side by side with the students. During year two, the gardens developed a bug and worm problem, so teachers asked one of the local nurseries and a home improvement store if they knew what was wrong. The nursery provided free fertilizer for the problem and also offered seeds and plants for the following year. The home improvement store offered to become a full partner in the school's service learning efforts. They visited the school, saw their existing gardens, and then worked with the school to build above-ground planters with an irrigation system. They even provided a small greenhouse for the seedlings and smaller plants donated by the local nursery. With the help of the nursery and the home improvement store, each of the school's classrooms had a bi-weekly checklist of responsibilities pertaining to the garden. The students learned about soil, planting, fertilizer, growing seasons, working with others, homelessness, and giving, and their teachers made strong connections to state standards.

half the year, and sometimes for a full year, before developing a school-wide focus. Some of the questions and topics the SLC deals with include:

1. What community effort will the school support or become partners in? A long-term, school-wide service learning effort has to be fairly broad in order to meet the needs of all the grade levels and sustain itself the whole year.

2. How does this effort fit with the school's mission statement? How will the school communicate this new service learning focus to parents, students, and the community?

3. Who are the community partners and what are their potential roles and contributions to the service learning effort? Meet with them and find out what resources they are willing to offer and how the school could become their partner in service learning.

4. Create a timeline for service learning implementation with roles and responsibilities for each classroom or grade level.

5. Determine the key social skills addressed for each grade level.

6. List the state standards and objectives to be taught via service learning so that every teacher understands the curricular integration of service learning in his or her individual content area.

Chapter Summary

As we work with preservice and in-service teachers, they continually ask us to provide a guideline, flowchart, template, checklist—*something*—to help them implement service learning in their classrooms. Our hope is that this chapter has offered such a tool. However, this chapter is only a starting place. As your service learning knowledge and experience evolves, you'll surely modify and integrate curriculum in ways that we haven't thought of. And as you create novel ways of planning, reflecting, documenting, mentoring, and celebrating, you contribute to the evolution of service learning in early childhood education.

PART TWO

Project Forms and Templates

Chapter 5

Planning Forms

Preparing for Service Learning

The following pages are useful for when you are preparing for the service learning project or activity. Use these pages in your preplanning stage:

- **Student Artifact Release Form** (page 40). As soon as you know the details of your service learning project, it is a good idea to have a release form ready to send out to the parents of the students. Student artifacts include any type of created product, such as cards, brochures, drawings, etc.

- **Student Photo Release Form** (page 41). Keep in mind that you cannot share a picture, put a picture on a website, or even include it in a teaching portfolio with the intention of sharing it with others, unless you have a signed release form from the parent or guardian of every child in the photo.

Brainstorming and Introducing Service Learning

These next forms are helpful for brainstorming and introducing the service learning activity to your students. Make them your own by adding, deleting, or modifying language to better suit your needs.

- **Brainstorming the Activity** (pages 42–43) is a "who, what, when, where, why" form that can be used at any level. Fill out this form with your students in small groups or as a whole group activity.

- **Beginning to Serve** (pages 44–45). This form provides guided questions to be answered about the service learning project. Fill out this form with your students in small groups or as a whole group activity.

- **Starting Something in Your Community** (pages 46–47) is a list of guided questions tailored to the needs of your community. Fill out this form with your students in small groups or as a whole group activity.

- **Preparing Students for Service** (page 48) provides a list of helpful ideas for working with students in order to better prepare them for service learning.

- **The ABCs of Service Learning** (page 49) is a good form to use at the beginning of your project to remind yourself what you need to do: **A**ssess, **B**rainstorm, and **C**onnect. You might find other documents more useful for recording details about each of the three areas, but this one is great for initial note-taking or brainstorming.

Organizational Forms

These three forms will help keep you and your service learning project organized. You also might want to think about creative ways to incorporate calendars, checklists, and tables as service learning tools.

- **Curriculum Connections: Preschool** (blank form, pages 50–51; example form, pages 52–53) and **Curriculum Connections: Primary Grades** (blank form, pages 54–55; example form, pages 56–57). Similar to a thematic web, these curriculum frameworks ask you to put your service learning project title in the middle and then make the curricular connections in the corresponding sections. The preschool framework uses more developmental domain language (expressive arts, dramatic play); the primary framework uses traditional content language (reading, math, social studies, etc.).

- **Curricular Skills Checklist** (page 58). This checklist can be used several different ways:

  1. List the skills of the service learning activity across the top of the form and list the students' name down the left side. Check them off as you say them or as they were mastered.

  2. List the skills across the top of the form and the curriculum or domain areas (math, science, expressive arts, dramatic play, etc.) down the left side.

  3. Combine the skills and curricular or domain areas across the top of the form, but group them together so, for example, all the dramatic play skills are together and all literacy skills are together (perhaps highlight each curricular or domain area in a different color). Then list the student's names down the left side.

- **Community Contacts** (pages 59–60). This form helps you keep track of all of your community partners. You can also modify it to keep track of parent information.

Overview and Planning

Use these forms as lesson plan formats and information sharing documents with stakeholders such as administration staff, community partners, and parents.

- **Service Learning Project Overview** (pages 61–62) provides a one-page summary of the project.

- **Service Learning Lesson Plan** (pages 63–64). When thinking about a service learning project or activity, this detailed lesson plan is usually the most helpful. See examples in Part 3, pages 118–161.

- **General Lesson Plan for Service Learning** (pages 65–66). This lesson plan format is more traditional and probably more familiar to you. We have included one with tips to show our thinking in each of the categories.

- **Ready, Set, Serve!** (pages 69–70) and **Teacher Expectations** (pages 71–72). These teacher planning forms are useful once the service learning project has been decided. The questions are thorough and a great way for you to prepare for the project.

- **Service Learning Action Plan** (pages 73–74). Use this form with your class to gather ideas about community issues, much like the **Starting Something in Your Community** tool (pages 46–47). Or, use it as a planning document once the service learning project is decided upon; these questions will help move the project forward to further aid the community.

Student Artifact Release Form

I hereby grant permission to _____

to use the work of my child _____

to promote a service learning project. I understand my child's artifacts (cards, brochures, drawings, etc.) may be used for academic purposes, such as class presentations and posters, and may be published on a school or community website, or in a newsletter, newspaper, or related materials.

Signature _____ Date _____

Print Name _____

Street Address _____

City _____ State _____ Zip _____

Email _____ Phone _____

> **Service learning** is a class assignment in which students apply curriculum concepts to a community need. Students address the need inside and/or outside of class and then reflect on and demonstrate for others how their service relates to the curriculum.

Student Photo Release Form

I hereby grant permission to _____

to take photographs or videos of my child _____

to promote a service learning project. I understand that the photographs or video taken of my child

are the property of _____

and may be used for academic purposes, such as class presentations and posters, and may be

published on a school or community website, or in a newsletter, newspaper, or related materials.

Signature _____ Date _____

Print Name _____

Street Address _____

City _____ State _____ Zip _____

Email _____ Phone _____

Service learning is a class assignment in which students apply curriculum concepts to a community need. Students address the need inside and/or outside of class and then reflect on and demonstrate for others how their service relates to the curriculum.

Brainstorming the Activity: A Framework for Service

1. What is service?

2. Why is service needed?

3. Who will we serve?

4. Why will we serve this cause?

5. How will we serve?

6. What will we need to serve?

continued ➡

7. Who will help us serve?

8. When will we serve?

9. Where will we serve?

10. How will we reflect on our service?

11. How will we thank those involved in serving?

12. What will we do to celebrate our service?

Beginning to Serve:
An Introduction to the Service Activity

Describe your service learning project or activity:

Describe what prompted you to choose this topic (e.g., book, video, current event, website, newspaper article):

What do you know about the problem or concern?

How does it make you feel?

continued ➡

What can you do about it?

How will that action help?

What might you learn along the way?

Starting Something in Your Community

What We Need

Make a list of concerns/needs that are present in your community.

1.

2.

3.

Explore a Concern

Community Concern:

- What causes it?

continued ➡

- List the people involved.

- Is anyone doing anything about it? If so, who?

- What are they doing? Is it helping? Why or why not?

- How could their actions be more helpful? If nothing is being done, what could be done to help?

- What resources are or would be needed? (List possible sources or suppliers of resources.)

Preparing Students for Service Learning

Working with students prior to the beginning of the project via learning activities, orientation, training, discussions, and stories, as well as throughout the service experience, will pay dividends in the end.

Here are some ideas:

- Read stories about service and caring to help children see the world from other people's perspectives.

- Participate in a special training or orientation. For students in preK–K, this might involve teaching a particular skill related to the project, such as how to plant flower seeds or make a greeting card.

- Read relevant newspapers, magazines, websites, textbooks, novels, or storybooks.

- Conduct research online, in the community, or in textbooks. For very young students, you might organize a simple field trip into the community or show them child-friendly interactive websites devoted to the topic you plan to address.

- Survey the community, faculty, or school. If you have a preschool or kindergarten class, you might visit another classroom to ask the students questions, or invite several teachers, school staff members, community members, or parents to visit your class so the children may ask them questions.

- Interview community members about their ideas and concerns for the community. Invite members to come to your class in person, if possible, especially if your children are very young.

- Listen to a guest speaker or attend an assembly.

- Plan the project: make a timeline, assign responsibilities, and gather materials. For students in preK–K, this might involve drawing pictures of activities and items needed, and enlisting parents' help in gathering materials.

- Create a budget and generate funds. This idea may not be appropriate for preschoolers or kindergartners.

- Recruit others to help, including peers and community members. Very young children can take invitations to help home to their parents.

- Develop a public relations campaign. In the earliest grades, this might be as simple as having the children make drawings or a large poster about their project to hang in the school hallway or cafeteria.

Adapted from A. Shoemaker, *Teaching Young Children Through Service: A Practical Guide for Understanding and Practicing Service-Learning with Children Ages 4 through 8.* St. Paul, MN: National Youth Leadership Council, 1999.

The ABCs of Service Learning

Assess the need or concern:

Brainstorm possible service solutions:

Connect the activity to the curriculum:

Curriculum Connections: Preschool

Literacy (e.g., books, poems)	Standards, Benchmarks, Objectives	Dramatic Play
Math & Science (e.g, sand and water, blocks, construction, manipulatives)	**Service Learning Activity:**	**Expressive Arts** (e.g., songs, finger plays, drama, art, movement)
Health, Safety & Community	**Social & Emotional Connections**	**Reflection Activity**

continued

Modifications & Accommodations:

Technology Uses:

Evaluation:

Celebration:

Curriculum Connections: Preschool

Literacy (e.g., books, poems) • Show picture cards of helpful behaviors. • Read children's book on occupations and helping others.	**Standards, Benchmarks, Objectives** • Identify support people in the school and their helpful behaviors. • Plan and implement monthly appreciation events. • Identify and web people's emotions and responses to the appreciation events.	**Dramatic Play** • Use materials that represent the support people. • Role-play the appreciation events.
Math & Science (e.g, sand and water, blocks, construction, manipulatives) • Using the pictures of each support person and a calendar page for each month in the school year, plan the appreciation events for the whole year. • Stress concepts of time, one-to-one ratio, and correspondence.	**Service Learning Activity:** Appreciation of Others	**Expressive Arts** (e.g., songs, finger plays, drama, art, movement) • Create new lyrics to recognized songs, teach them to the children, and sing at the appreciation events (see example at end). • Create appreciation cards for each support person.
Health, Safety & Community • Focus on each support person's efforts as part of the school community. • Include safety and health elements of each support member's position.	**Social & Emotional Connections** • Make appreciation connections to children's literature. • Use reflection activity to discuss emotions and helpful behaviors.	**Reflection Activity** • Keep a growing appreciation web that the class will add to after each event. This will help them make connections between their feelings about each event, the participant's feelings, and their impact on others in their school community.

continued

Curriculum Connections: Preschool (continued)

Modifications & Accommodations:

Based on the religious and ethnic makeup of classroom children, appreciation events may need to be modified. For example, if families don't celebrate birthdays, ongoing appreciation events should not include singing "Happy Birthday" and making birthday cards.

Technology Uses:

- Using clip art, card templates, etc., create appreciation cards for each event.
- Play and record music to accompany each appreciation event.
- Make a CD to present to each support person at his or her appreciation event; include the appreciation song and audio of a class discussion about how that person is helpful and why students need to show appreciation to others.

Evaluation:

- Throughout the year, invite previous appreciation event recipients to talk to the class about what it meant to them to be appreciated.
- Use the final appreciation web (see reflection activity) to discuss children's feelings about each event and the impact of their project on others in the school community.
- Children represent what they learned from the project by making up a song, drawing a picture, etc.

Celebration:

- Each appreciation event is a celebration. At the end of the year, plan a culminating celebration with all support staff.

Example of appreciation song: (sing to tune of "Twinkle, Twinkle Little Star")

"Thank you, thank you very much,
For the work you do for us.
Without you our school would be,
Not as [clean] (insert word for each support person) as it can be.
Thank you, thank you very much,
For the work you do for us."

Curriculum Connections:
Primary Grades

Language Arts	Standards, Benchmarks, Objectives	Social Studies
Math	Service Learning Activity:	Fine Arts
Science & Health	Social & Emotional Connections	Reflection Activity

continued

Modifications & Accommodations:

Technology Uses:

Evaluation:

Celebration:

Curriculum Connections:
Primary Grades

Language Arts	Standards, Benchmarks, Objectives	Social Studies
• Read fiction and nonfiction books about flags and the military.	• Identify components of the U.S. flag, history of flag, and its corresponding symbolism. • Create a quilt square for class quilt. • Identify characteristics of good citizenship. • Identify military symbols and the role of the military in our country today.	• Study the history of the flag. • Study the flag's elements and corresponding symbolism. • Learn the geography of deployed troops. • Learn the purpose of the military.
Math	**Service Learning Activity:**	**Fine Arts**
• Compare and contrast U.S. flags over time. • Match U.S. flags to colony/state configurations. • Chart number of troops deployed each year since 2000.	Flag for Our Troops	• Each child creates a quilt square (first on paper then on fabric) that is unique and symbolic using what they learned about the military, citizenship, and the flag.
Science & Health	**Social & Emotional Connections**	**Reflection Activity**
• Focus on mental health and discuss how being deployed can make a person feel. • Make connections to how the children feel when being good citizens in school and the community.	• Identify a community need and behaviors associated with volunteerism by participating in a service learning project for the military. • Identify and demonstrate examples of good citizenship by decorating a flag square with a note written to the soldiers on the back.	• Make connections between flag symbols, citizenship, and military service. • Children discuss how making the quilt is an example of good citizenship.

continued

Curriculum Connections: Primary Grades (continued)

Modifications & Accommodations:

- Provide visuals and support to explain flag symbolism.
- Role-play scenarios to illustrate concepts of citizenship.

Technology Uses:

- Design personal flag squares using computers.
- Do an Internet search for U.S. symbols and flag symbols to use for the quilt squares.

Evaluation:

- Determine if the children are able to correctly match flag elements with symbols.
- Ask if the children can identify their behaviors during the project and tell how they were examples
of being a good citizen.

Celebration:

- Share the class flag with the school and community and tell how the service learning project was an
example of good citizenship.
- Hang paper version of class flag in school or community (grocery store, public library, veteran's center,
hospital, etc.).
- Once it has arrived at destination, share pictures with children of the flag with the troops, if possible.

Curricular Skills Checklist

Student Name or Domain Area	Skill and/or Domain Area							

Community Contacts

Organization Name	Address	Phone Number	Email	Contact Person(s)	Date	Notes
						59

continued ➡

Who can help with advertising the event?
(for example, local radio or TV stations, newspapers, websites, school bulletins, store windows, community bulletin boards, etc.)

Who might help with materials and resources?
(for example, office supply stores, home centers, supermarkets, etc.)

Service Learning Project Overview

Community Need:

Service Goal:

Learning Outcomes:

Curriculum Connections

❑ Language Arts   ❑ Fine Arts   ❑ Technology

❑ Mathematics   ❑ Social Studies   ❑ Character Education

❑ Science   ❑ Health   ❑

How connected?

Service Delivery

Estimated Start Date: Estimated Completion Date:

Resources Needed:

Preparation:

Tasks to Complete Service:

continued ➡

Parental Involvement Activity:

Special Activities:

Demonstration:

Methods of Reflection:

Celebration (date/activity):

Service Learning Lesson Plan

Teacher: Grade:

Project Name:

Purpose/Goal: How will this project help others in the community?

Need: Why is this project needed and how will it be integrated with the existing curriculum?

Curriculum Objectives: What are the curriculum objectives the students will learn as a result of participating in this service learning project?

Social/Character Objectives: What are the social/character objectives the students will learn as a result of participating in this service learning project?

Participation: Who will help and what will they do?

Students:

Teachers:

Community Partners and Other Adults:

continued ➡

Adapted from C. B. Kaye, *The Complete Guide to Service Learning: Proven, Practical Ways to Engage Students in Civic Responsibility, Academic Curriculum, and Social Action.* Minneapolis, MN: Free Spirit Publishing, 2010. Used with permission.

Service Learning Lesson Plan (continued)

Planning and Action: What type of planning will take place before and during the service learning project? What specific teacher and student learning experiences are planned (based on the needs, purpose, objectives, and participants)?

Reflection: What types of reflection are planned throughout the service learning experience and when will they happen?

Outcomes/Evaluations: What evidence or products will be collected throughout and at the end of the project? (include curricular *and* social outcomes)

Resources: What is needed to get the job done? (itemize supplies, materials, resources, contacts, etc.)

Documentation: How will the learning gained from the service learning project be shared with others?

Celebration: How will the service learning project and learning be celebrated?

Adapted from C. B. Kaye, *The Complete Guide to Service Learning: Proven, Practical Ways to Engage Students in Civic Responsibility, Academic Curriculum, and Social Action.* Minneapolis, MN: Free Spirit Publishing, 2010. Used with permission.

General Lesson Plan for Service Learning

Teacher:

Grade Level:

Curriculum or Domain Standards:

Social/Character Skills:

Outline of Procedures

Teacher Activity

Be detailed—what are you going to do to make sure that the objectives are being taught? Remember that social skills are taught, too, not just the curricular skills. List your questions, what kinds of grouping you will use, etc.

Student Activity

How will students demonstrate they have learned the objectives?

continued

General Lesson Plan for Service Learning (continued)

Outline of Procedures

Opening Activity/Set	Lesson Objectives	Closure	Method of Evaluation
Use brainstorming or story ideas to set the stage for your service learning activity and get everyone excited!	*Be specific about the curriculum skills and social/character skills the students will learn as part of the service learning project.*	*How will students process all or part of the lesson objectives?*	*How will you know the children have learned each lesson objective?*

Materials: *List your materials here; be very specific because memory is not a good tool to rely on in lesson planning!*

General Lesson Plan for Service Learning

Teacher: **Mrs. Swanson**

Curriculum or Domain Standards: **Social Studies, the Arts, Math**

Social/Character Skills: **Citizenship, Service to Others, Helping, Support, Friendship**

Grade Level: **2**

Outline of Procedures

Teacher Activity

- Explain the service learning project to the children.
- Read books and lead discussions on military citizenship, and the U.S. flag.
- Create and show visuals of flag elements and corresponding symbols for math matching activity (usflag.org/colors.html).
- Help children make connections between flag symbols, citizenship, and military service.
- Outline procedures for each quilt square and discuss how making the quilt is an example of good citizenship.
- Make quilt when all the squares are finished.
- Document the service learning project at each stage.

Student Activity

- Participate in class discussion about what the military is and what it means to be in the military.
- Draw possible connections between military service and being a good citizen in school and community.
- Talk and read about the U.S. flag.
- Make a class flag. Each student will decorate a square that is unique and symbolic using what he or she learned about the military, citizenship, and the flag. Then, the student will write a "Thank You for _____" and sign his or her name on the back of the square

continued

General Lesson Plan for Service Learning (continued)

Outline of Procedures

Opening Activity/Set	Lesson Objectives	Closure	Method of Evaluation
Invite a guest speaker—a member of the military or military family—to introduce what the military does, discuss deployment and being away from family, and how she or he sees how being a member of the military is being a good citizen.	• Identify components of the U.S. flag, history of flag, and its corresponding symbolism. • Create a quilt square for class quilt. • Identify characteristics of good citizenship. • Identify military symbols and the role of the military in our country today. • Identify need and behaviors associated with community volunteers by participating in a service learning Project for the military. • Identify and demonstrate examples of good citizenship by decorating a square of fabric with a note on the back written to the soldiers.	• First closure will be when the children make connections between flag symbols, citizenship, and military service. • Second closure will be when the children discuss how making the quilt is an example of good citizenship.	Complete a checklist: ☐ The student correctly matched flag elements with symbols. ☐ The student correctly discussed symbols used on his or her quilt squares and why the symbols are important to him or her and to the military. ☐ The student correctly identified characteristics of good citizens and how she or he showed good citizenship in the service learning Project

Materials:

Fiction and nonfiction flag and military books; books illustrating children being good citizens and what citizenship looks like; Pictures matching flag elements with symbolism (usflag.org/colors.html); 8" × 6" paper squares and fabric squares (estimate 1 1/2 squares per child to account for do-overs); fabric markers or Paint; military address; camera to document Project

Ready, Set, Serve!
Teacher Planning Form

1. Service activity idea:

2. Benefits to the community:

3. Benefits to the students:

4. Connections to the curriculum:

5. Standards or benchmarks to be addressed:

6. Materials needed to introduce and complete the activity:

continued

7. Possible community partners:

8. Parental involvement possibilities:

9. Ways to get the word out:

10. Evaluation procedures:

11. Reflection process:

12. Celebration ideas:

Teacher Expectations: Planning the Service Learning Experience

I have chosen this activity to extend or complement our study of:

I will address the following community concern with my students:

I will use the following resources to introduce the concept:

I will encourage students to seek service solutions to community concerns by:

Developmentally appropriate aspects of this project are:

I will involve the parents by:

I will involve others in the community by:

continued ➡

I will discuss with students:

I will assess learning outcomes by:

We will reflect on our service experience in the following ways:

We will celebrate our involvement by:

As a result of this service experience, I hope the students are impacted in the following ways:

Planning Notes:

Service Learning Action Plan

What are the needs in our school or community?

How can we learn more about these needs?

Is anyone already helping? How?

What can we do?

How will this help?

continued ➡

What will we need?

How will we obtain these resources?

Who will we contact?

Will we need assistance?

When will we get started?

Chapter 6

Community Partner Forms

Community Member Release Forms

These are management forms for your community partners. They may have their own agreement and release forms, just ask them. There is no need to duplicate the agreement form, however, your school name must be on the photo agreement form for liability purposes if your school or students plan to share any photo showing a community member or student.

- **Community Member Photo Release Form** (page 76) and **Community Member Artifact Release Form** (page 77). A good general rule of thumb: *Do* not *take a picture or video of a person or share any of that person's original work unless he or she has turned in a release form.*

School Contact Information

These forms provide helpful organization information to the community partners in case they need to contact the school.

- **School Contact Log** (page 78). This form will help the community partner keep track of contacts they have with the school.

- **School Roles and Contact Information** (page 79). This form should be filled out by each individual school and provided to the community partner so he or she is clear about everyone's role and knows who to contact.

Evaluation

When evaluating the service learning project, do not forget your community partners! They often have valuable insights that can move your service learning to a whole new level.

- **Community Partner Evaluation of Service Learning and Student Helpers** (pages 80–81). This two-page survey asks the community partners to evaluate how satisfied they are with the specific service learning project and student helpers. It uses a four-point Lickert scale ranging from "Strongly Disagree" to "Strongly Agree." The criteria can be modified or tailored to better fit your specific program and the ages of your students. *Note:* This form may not be appropriate for use with very young children.

Community Member
Photo Release Form

I hereby grant permission to _____

to take photographs or videos of _____

to promote a service learning project. I understand that the photographs or videos taken of me are

the property of _____

and may be used for academic purposes, such as class presentations and posters, and may be

published on a school or community website, or in a newsletter, newspaper, or related materials.

Signature _____ Date _____
                            (Parent/Guardian if under age 18)

Print Name _____

Street Address _____

City _____ State _____ Zip _____

Email _____ Phone _____

Service learning is a class assignment in which students apply curriculum concepts to a community need. Students address the need inside and/or outside of class and then reflect on and demonstrate for others how their service relates to the curriculum.

Community Member Artifact Release Form

I hereby grant permission to _____
to use my work to promote a service learning project. I understand my artifacts (original creative products) may be used for academic purposes, such as class presentations and posters, and may be published on a school or community website, or in a newsletter, newspaper, or related materials.

Signature _____ Date _____
(Parent/Guardian if under age 18)

Print Name _____

Street Address _____

City _____ State _____ Zip _____

Email _____ Phone _____

Service learning is a class assignment in which students apply curriculum concepts to a community need. Students address the need inside and/or outside of class and then reflect on and demonstrate for others how their service relates to the curriculum.

School Contact Log

Date of Contact	School Name & Address	Phone	Email	Contact Person(s)	Notes

School Roles and Contact Information

Name	Email	Phone	Role

Community Partner Evaluation of Service Learning and Student Helpers

Name: Date:

Agency:

Directions: Thank you for working with us and hosting our students! Please help us better serve you by answering the following questions. Check the appropriate box.

	Strongly Agree	Agree	Disagree	Strongly Disagree	N/A
Your student volunteers ("service learners") have augmented my agency's service delivery. They do meaningful work!					
There has been sufficient communication between your school and our agency.					
Overall, the students have been dedicated and committed to their volunteer work.					
Service learners and staff have worked together effectively.					
Students generally stay long enough to help my agency.					
Students generally have the skills and abilities to fulfill volunteer tasks and responsibilities.					
Students are an important part of our volunteer program.					
I would like more contact with or participation from your school faculty/staff.					

continued ➡

Community Partner Evaluation of Service Learning and Student Helpers (continued)

	Strongly Agree	Agree	Disagree	Strongly Disagree	N/A
The amount of agency supervisory time with students is about right.					
I would like to utilize more technical resources, e.g., information about effective use of service learners.					
Overall, I am satisfied with your school's service learners.					
Overall, I am satisfied with the experience provided by your school.					

How would you improve the service learning program?

How has your agency benefited by utilizing student service learners?

How have students benefited from their experiences with your organization?

Other comments, suggestions, or recommendations?

Chapter 7

Reflection and Documentation Forms

> *Note:* The star bullets denote forms to use with children. With younger students, you can fill out the forms as a group.

Reflection Ideas

These two forms are ideas for reflection for both students and teachers involved with service learning.

- ★ **Service Learning Reflection Activity** (pages 84–85). This form includes 12 different prompts that you can use with children in any service learning activity. Use these prompts for whole group discussion, small group discussion, or as a brainstorming activity. Have children record their answers via writing or drawing—alone or with a partner, or by role-playing. Read the prompts aloud to very young children.

- • **Service Learning Teacher Reflection Ideas** (pages 86–87). These questions are tailored for preservice teachers and ask them to reflect on their students' engagement in the service learning experience. (See Chapter 14 for more information on service learning with preservice teachers.)

Connecting Knowledge and Feelings

The following five documents are powerful tools. Not only do they connect knowledge and feelings with the service learning project, but they do so by using basic graphic organizers. The first is a reflection tool, and the remaining documents are both reflection and documentation tools.

- ★ **Service Learning KWL Chart** (page 88) is a traditional KWL chart. KWL stands for what the student *knows,* what the student *wants* to know, and what the student has *learned* about a topic. Have your students look closely at the descriptors and write or draw their responses in the spaces provided. Read the descriptors aloud to very young children and fill out the chart as a class. This tool can be used with students throughout the service learning project to assess new learning along the way. After completing their charts, ask children how they can share them with others, making this tool both reflection and documentation.

- ★ **Service Learning KFL Chart** (page 89) is a modified KWL chart in which the "F" stands for how the children *feel* about the problem they are addressing in their service learning project.

- ★ **Service Learning Postcard Reflection** (page 90) is a great way for children to reflect on their service learning project and share what they have learned with others. Have them describe what their class did for a project, how the project made them feel, and what they learned while completing the project. Be sure to have them illustrate the reverse side before mailing!

★ **Service Learning Friendly Letter Planning Form** (page 91) is similar to the postcard reflection, but longer. Students' letters can also be used in the investigation and preparation stages of service learning. Consider having your children write to community members asking for help or for materials. Letters can be traditional pen-and-paper or emails. If you teach very young children, have them express their thoughts using pictures, while you add the text.

★ **Service Learning Friendly Letter Planning Web** (page 92) can help students plan what they will write or draw in their letters.

Ongoing Reflection Ideas

These reflection strategies are intended to be ongoing and often carry over into multiple days, which will enable you to engage in more reflection.

★ **Service Learning ABC Reflection** (blank form, page 93; example form, page 94). Have children recall and connect information to a word, phrase, or picture that must begin with a particular letter of the alphabet. Children can work individually, in pairs, in small groups, or even as a whole group. Variations include using the letters S-E-R-V-I-C-E L-E-A-R-N-I-N-G, or the name of or main word from a project, such as R-E-C-Y-C-L-E or W-H-A-L-E-S.

★ **Service Learning Alphabet Book** (no handout necessary). Each child creates a page with three things (writings and/or drawings) they learned about from participating in the project that begin with a specific letter, such as "**A** is for animals, advocacy, affection." So each page will hold several reflections and the book itself would become part of the documentation of the service learning project.

★ **Service Learning Four-Square Reflection** (no handout necessary). Each child or pair of children will need an 18" x 12" sheet of construction paper folded in fourths (fold the short ends together, then the long ends together). In each quadrant of the paper, the child or pair of

children will respond to your service learning reflection prompts. Use the **Service Learning Reflection Activity** prompts (page 84–85) or create your own. Each prompt should be fairly involved, so completion of this entire reflection will need a minimum of four days.

★ **Service Learning Log** (pages 95–96). Children respond to the service learning process through journal entries. Students draw or write on the handout (or in their journals) responding to your prompts. The handout includes suggested questions.

★ **Service Learning Chain of Events** (blank form, page 97; example form, page 98). This graphic organizer allows children to follow the process of the service learning project and to isolate critical information. Have children reflect on four different events in the order they occurred.

★ **Service Learning Hand Chart** (page 99) and **Service Learning Spider Chart** (blank form, page 100; example form, page 101) are graphic organizers that ask factual questions (Who? What? Where? When? Why? How? What if?) about the service learning project. Students can answer with phrases, sentences, or drawings.

★ **Service Learning Reflection Envelope** (no handout necessary). During the service learning project, tape envelopes to the top of the board or somewhere else prominently in the classroom. Inside each envelope, include a reflection question or activity. At the appropriate time each day during the service learning lesson, have a child or the class choose which envelope to open, and then they complete the reflection activity inside.

Documenting the Learning

• **Documentation Ideas** (page 102) suggests several ways for you and your students to share with others what you have learned from the service learning experience. These ideas are just a starting place; be creative, think outside the box, and document your service learning in unique and unusual ways!

Service Learning Reflection Activity

Name:_____ Date:_____

I learned that . . .

Learning this made me feel . . .

Helping others made me feel . . .

The best part of the project was . . .

We can make this project better next time by . . .

continued

Service Learning Reflection Activity ^(continued)

My role in this project was . . .

Another way I would like to help is . . .

Our class chose this project because . . .

I hope that the people we served . . .

Students should get involved with service learning projects because . . .

Service Learning
Teacher Reflection Ideas

Please describe the impact of this project on you and the impact on your students. Some things to ponder and write about:

Why was this project important to you and the kids?

What types of learning experiences did your students do that were the same or different from their regular curriculum?

How engaged were your students?

continued ➡

Did students who often get into trouble do so during this project? Why or why not?

What teacher strategies did you use that were the same or different from teaching the regular curriculum?

Service Learning KWL Chart

Name:_____ Date:_____

What I KNOW about the problem	What I WANT to know about the problem	What I have LEARNED about the problem

Service Learning KFL Chart

Name:_____ Date:_____

What I KNOW about the problem	How I FEEL about the problem	What I hope to LEARN from the project

Service Learning Postcard Reflection

_____ _____, 20_____

Dear _____,

Our class . . .

It made me feel . . .

I learned . . .

Thanks for reading!

                              Your Friend,

                              _____

Service Learning Friendly Letter Planning Form

_____ _____, 20_____

Dear _____,

I helped my community by . . .

I learned that . . .

This made me feel . . .

Questions I have are . . .

Your Friend,

_____

Service Learning Friendly Letter Planning Web

Name:_____ Date:_____

| How I helped my community: | What I have learned: |

My service learning project:

| How it made me feel: | Questions I have: |

Service Learning ABC Reflection

Name:_____ Date:_____

S_____   L_____

E_____   E_____

R_____   A_____

V_____   R_____

I_____   N_____

C_____   I_____

E_____   N_____

                               G_____

Service Learning ABC Reflection

Name: _Kira_   Date: _September 20_

S _Safety_   **L** _Listen to TV or radio_

E _Emergency_   **E** _Evacuate_

R _Rescue_   **A** _Alarm_

V _Volunteer_   **R** _Rainstorm_

I _Inland_   **N** _Natural disasters_

C _Community_   **I** _Inside (stay inside)_

E _Eye of the storm_   **N** _Names of hurricanes_

     G _Gusts_

Service Learning Log

Name:_____ Date:_____

1. What was one important thing you learned about the service learning project today?

2. What helped you learn in today's class?

3. What do you enjoy most about helping others?

continued

4. How does helping others make you feel?

5. What new information did you learn from today's lesson or discussion?

6. How well are you working with others in class on the service learning project?

7. Think of your own question. Write it and then answer it.

Service Learning Chain of Events

Name:_____ Date:_____

1.

2.

3.

4.

Service Learning Chain of Events

Name: _Lindsey_   Date: _September 20_

1.

We learned about hurricanes.

2.

I read a book about hurricanes.

3.

Our group made a poster for hurricane safety.

4.

We showed our poster and talked about hurricane safety with other kids.

Service Learning Hand Chart

Name:_____ Date:_____

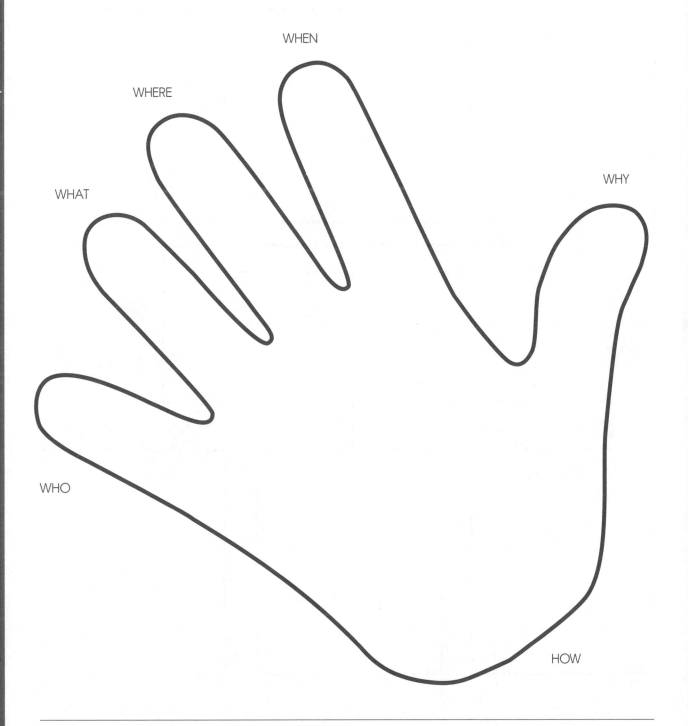

WHEN

WHERE

WHY

WHAT

WHO

HOW

Service Learning Spider Chart

Name:_____ Date:_____

Who?	What?	Where?

My service learning project:

When?	Why?	What if?

Service Learning Spider Chart

Name: __Gabriel_____   Date: __September 20_____

Who?
my class
my teacher
cafeteria workers
cleaning people
office people

What?
We made thank-you cards and flower pens.

Where?
We made the cards and pens in our class. We took them to the people who work in our school.

My service learning project:

Saying Thank You with Flowers

When?
We did it after our science class.

Why?
We wanted to tell all the people thank you because they work so hard.

What if?
What if some people don't use pens?
We could make them something else instead.

Documentation Ideas

Below are some documentation ideas that can be used with young children. Check the ideas you might want to use to document your service learning project.

❏ Role-play (do a one-act play of) a particular scene or interaction from the service learning project.

❏ Spread the news by putting the information in the school's newsletter, newspaper, or website, and/or talking on the morning announcements or school radio station.

❏ Make posters describing your project and distribute them around the school and/or community (library, grocery stores, community centers, etc.).

❏ Write a letter to the editor of the local paper describing the service need and what your class did to help.

❏ Write letters or cards to government agencies or officials and local businesses describing the service need and what your class did to help. Ask them to join also!

❏ Raise awareness in your school by informing other classes of the service need and what your class did to help.

❏ Write a song and perform it at a school assembly.

❏ Write a poem and recite it at a school assembly or over the school's morning announcements.

❏ Make a scrapbook page and publish it in the school yearbook.

❏ Create a video and post it on your school's website.

❏ Make a class book and shelve it in your library.

❏ Other:

Notes:

Chapter 8

Assessment and Evaluation Forms

> *Note:* The star bullets denote forms to use with children. With younger students, you can fill out the forms as a group.

Assessments with Children

When we started working in the area of early childhood service learning, we searched for assessments or evaluations to use, but we could not find any. So we went back to what we know works with young children and used those principles for the following documents.

★ **Child-to-Child Evaluation of Service Learning** (pages 104–105) is an evaluation that consists of seven questions your students will ask each other about their service learning project. Make the questions more specific to your age level and project, or add additional questions if you wish.

★ **Service Learning Smiley Evaluation** (blank form, page 106; example form, page 107) is an open-ended service learning Lickert scale that uses smiley faces. Have the children write in the criteria that you want to evaluate, and/ or read it aloud to the children, and have them color in their answers.

★ **Service Learning Portrait Assessment** (page 108). Children love this creative way to think about the service learning experience, while at the same time telling how they accomplished the goals of the project. In each space, words and/or pictures can be used to communicate their understanding.

★ **Service Learning TOW Assessment** (blank form, pages 109–110; example form, pages 111–112). Fill in the four criteria, and then have the students evaluate each and state what was **T**errific, **O**kay, and needs **W**ork (TOW) about each. This evaluation makes a great cooperative learning activity and can even be done in pictures or acted out.

Teacher Service Learning Assessments

The following forms are for you, the teacher, to fill out upon completion of your service learning project. Keeping this information on record is important as you adjust projects and approaches going forward and also as you discuss tips and suggestions for service learning projects with other teachers or groups. You may wish to modify the forms slightly and give them to other project participants to fill out, such as community partners, parents, administrators, or other teachers.

• **Teacher Assessment of the Service Learning Project** (pages 113–114) is an overall evaluation of the project your class completed and how it impacted your students.

• **Teacher Assessment of the Service Learning Site or Partner Organization** (page 115) is a brief evaluation focusing on the community site or partner organization you worked with during your project. It asks for critical feedback about working with the partner and if you would recommend the partner to others.

Child-to-Child Evaluation
of Service Learning

Name:_____ Date:_____

1. What is your name and the title of your project?

2. Tell me about your service learning project.

3. What did you learn from this project that you didn't know before?

continued

4. How was your project helpful?

5. How did your project help other people, animals, or the environment?

6. What other things have you done to be helpful since working on your project?

7. How did working on this project compare to the rest of your schoolwork?

Thank you!

Service Learning Smiley Evaluation

Name:_____ Date:_____

Service Learning Project Title: _____

1. _____

Terrific   Okay   Needs Work

2. _____

Terrific   Okay   Needs Work

3. _____

Terrific   Okay   Needs Work

4. _____

Terrific   Okay   Needs Work

Service Learning Smiley Evaluation

Name: <u>Walt</u>   Date: <u>September 20</u>

Service Learning Project Title: <u>Hurricane Safety and Survival Kits</u>

1. <u>I know how to stay safe if a hurricane is coming.</u>

Terrific   Okay   Needs Work

2. <u>I know what goes in a hurricane safety kit.</u>

Terrific   Okay   Needs Work

3. <u>I can tell other people how to stay safe in a hurricane.</u>

Terrific   Okay   Needs Work

4. <u>I know what a hurricane is.</u>

Terrific   Okay   Needs Work

Service Learning Portrait Assessment

Name:_____ Date:_____

Look at me!
(draw your face here)

What was easy for me:

I was good at:

My project:

What was hard for me:

What I accomplished:

In the future, I'd like to:

Service Learning TOW Assessment

Name:_____ Date:_____

Service Learning Project Title:_____

1._____

Terrific:

Okay:

Work Needed:

2._____

Terrific:

Okay:

Work Needed:

continued ➡

3. _____

Terrific:

Okay:

Work Needed:

4. _____

Terrific:

Okay:

Work Needed:

Service Learning TOW Assessment

Name: <u>Marco</u>   Date: <u>September 20</u>

Service Learning Project Title: <u>Saying Thank You with Flowers</u>

1. <u>Made a list of people who worked at the school.</u>

Terrific: We made a really long list.

Okay: We couldn't remember some people's names.

Work Needed: We forgot some people.

2. <u>Made cards.</u>

Terrific: It was fun! I like doing art.

Okay: I wanted to paint my cards but we only got
to use markers.

Work Needed: My writing isn't so good.

continued

3. <u>Made flower pens.</u>

Terrific: They looked good.

Okay: We needed more pens. We had to wait for
the teacher to get more.

Work Needed: It was kind of hard. We had to help
each other.

4. <u>Handed out cards and flower pens.</u>

Terrific: I liked making everybody smile.

Okay: Two people weren't there so we had to leave them
on their desk.

Work Needed: I didn't get to hand out all the pens.
We had to take turns.

Teacher Assessment of the Service Learning Project

1. Describe your service learning project.

2. Describe the involvement of community members or organizations.

3. How effective was the project for your class?

4. How did your students benefit from the project?

5. What changes in students' knowledge and performance have occurred as a result of the project?

6. What changes in students' attitudes and behavior have occurred as a result of the project?

continued

7. What changes in students' enthusiasm or motivation have occurred as a result of the project?

8. Describe any changes in the ways that students talk about service learning or the subject area of their project.

9. Describe three specific student products and compare their quality with other work by those students.

10. How did this service learning project support the content standards and social curriculum?

11. What have been the major barriers to students participating in this service learning project?

12. Are you planning to use service learning again in your instruction?

Notes:

Teacher Assessment of the Service Learning Site or Partner Organization

1. Cite one example of how your class made an impact at your service learning site or with your community partner.

2. Explain how your class related and worked together with the community partner.

3. Explain what you particularly liked about working with this partner and what you would recommend be changed to enhance the experience.

4. Would you undertake another service learning project with this partner or recommend them to another class? Why or why not?

5. What other sites or partners would you like to work with in the future? List contact names and information.

Notes:

PART THREE

Sample Lesson Plans

Important Notes

- All sample lesson plans in Part Three are aligned with state and/or national academic learning standards. In the absence of national preK standards, projects involving preK students are aligned with the Head Start Framework as well as Florida PreK Performance Standards.

- Not every sample lesson plan includes identical information. The planning forms have undergone changes over the years, and some are more thorough than others and include student and/or teacher evaluations. However, each chapter includes at least one thorough lesson plan.

- See pages 205–207 for children's book and website recommendations that correspond to the lesson plans. See page 162 for a matrix listing all lesson plans by topic, grade level, and subject area, along with additional project ideas.

Chapter 9

Letter Writing Projects

Some of the simplest service learning projects that can be used with young children are those that involve communicating with others through letter writing. When young children write letters or cards for others, not only are they developing their writing skills, they are also placed in situations where they must consider the thoughts and feelings of other individuals. Through letter writing, children engage in authentic meaningful activities while often considering others who are in need. Letter writing projects might relate to a cause where children write letters to government officials or administrators. In doing so, children are rewarded not with a letter grade, but with the knowledge that they can make a difference. Children can also write letters to families or individuals who have been victims of natural disasters such as hurricanes or tornadoes. There is not a single community that does not have individuals who are in need, such as people in hospitals or senior citizens living in nursing or retirement homes. Writing letters or cards for these individuals can have a lasting impact on young children. Other letter writing projects could be directed toward supporting those who serve in the military, such as soldiers, or those whose occupation puts them in harm's way, such as firefighters.

For this chapter we have chosen sample lesson plans that are appropriate for each of the grade levels from preK to grade 3. Each lesson plan, however, could easily be adapted for other grade levels. All of the lesson plans were developed by early childhood teachers and have been used with young children in preschool through third grade. Each lesson plan includes information about the academic standards that are addressed, as well as instructional objectives. While some of the lesson plans have been modified for this text, the changes have been minimal. Note that all lesson plans are snapshots of larger projects that the children and their teachers had been engaged in over a period of time.

Sample Lesson Plan

Butterfly Cards for Seniors

Project Name: Spring for Seniors
Grade: PreK
Teacher: Leslie S.
Type of Service: Direct or Indirect

Purpose

If possible, visit a senior center or have seniors visit the school so the children can give the cards to them directly (direct service). If that is not possible, organize when and where to send the letters and how to make sure the seniors receive them and put them throughout the senior center for the residents to enjoy (indirect service).

Need

Senior centers love to have children send artwork to decorate rooms and hallways. This is a great way for my students to practice writing and to have fun creating bugs and springtime pictures to give to the senior center. Some seniors do not have visitors or letters sent to them, and this is a wonderful way to let them know there is someone who cares.

Resources and Materials:

- construction paper
- markers
- butterfly pattern
- lined paper for writing
- Eric Carle books

Standards

Head Start Framework
Literacy: Book Knowledge and Appreciation; Early Writing

Florida PreK Performance Standards
Language, Communication, and Emergent Literacy: Emergent Reading: Demonstrates comprehension of text read aloud

Language, Communication, and Emergent Literacy: Emergent Writing: Uses scribbling, letter-like shapes, and letters that are clearly different from drawing to represent thoughts and ideas; Demonstrates knowledge of purposes, functions, and structure of written composition

Student Academic Objectives

- Draw a picture of their favorite Eric Carle book.
- Dictate and/or write a sentence that goes with the picture of their favorite Eric Carle book.

Student Social Objectives

Delivering the cards to the seniors, the students will participate in giving to others and will, hopefully, experience the joy of the seniors and better understand issues of loneliness.

Planning and Action

- **Students:** They will write and draw pictures on butterfly-format cards. They will use invented spelling to "write" a sentence on the card, or they will dictate the sentence and I will write what they say using conventional spelling.

- **Teacher:** The other student teacher in the classroom will help me monitor card-making. I will look at the cards and work with the students to make sure they are readable for the seniors. Also, I'll provide various art supplies for them to make the cards.

Outcome

Using butterfly cards that resemble characters in Eric Carle books, the students will draw or "write" about the various Eric Carle books that they have been studying throughout the week. They will share their favorite book and why they liked it.

End Product

The end product will be the butterfly cards with the written/dictated sentence. Also, I will take pictures of the students making the cards to give to the senior center.

Sample Lesson Plan

Letters to Soldiers

Project Name: Letters to Soldiers
Grades: K and 1
Teachers: Susana E. and Dyana M.; Angela L.
Type of Service: Indirect

Purpose

First, this project will show how much the children have learned about the unit topic (space), so we can modify our teaching to better assist them. Second, it will create awareness about the war in Iraq. Third, it will allow the children to practice their writing skills in a fun and purposeful way.

Need

In two different classrooms, the children have been learning about space and flowers. Writing letters to soldiers will give them an opportunity to share what they have learned and help them practice their writing skills.

- **Space:** Since we couldn't think of any space service learning projects, we decided to have the children write what they learned about space on cards and send the cards to soldiers serving in Iraq.

Resources and Materials:

- paper (white or colored)
- crayons
- ribbon
- pencils
- stickers
- confetti
- an address for troops in Iraq

- **Flowers:** We learned that the tents the soldiers live in don't have many decorations to help them feel at home, so we wanted to send cards with flowers to say thank you and to serve as decorations for their tents.

Standards

Common Core State Standards

English Language Arts: Reading for Information; Key Ideas and Details

English Language Arts: Writing; Text Types and Purposes

National Science Standards

Earth Science: Objects in the Sky (for space focus)

Life Science: The Characteristics of Organisms (for flowers focus)

Student Academic Objectives

Write two facts about space or flowers and include a personal message to soldiers.

Student Social Objectives

Students will learn about the soldiers' duties in Iraq and that soldiers are sometimes away from their families for long periods of time. Sending letters is a way to show the soldiers that the students are grateful for what they are doing.

Planning and Action

- **Students:** They will start by participating in a discussion about what they know about the war in Iraq.

  Space focus: Students will write sentences stating what they have learned about while studying space. Next, they will write letters to soldiers, including at least one sentence about space and anything else they might want to add. Lastly, they will decorate their letters using markers, stickers, ribbon, confetti, and crayons.

  Flowers focus: Students will design a card depicting a flower. They will write one fact that they have learned about flowers on the first page of a letter to soldiers. They will then write a personal message to the troops where they can say "Thank you" or "We appreciate what you do."

- **Teachers:** We will start the class by asking the students if they know anything about the war in Iraq. We'll let them know that they will be writing letters to soldiers, telling them what they learned while studying space or flowers. Mrs. W. will come in and show pictures of her husband who is in the service and talk to the kids about what he does. We'll ask the children to state some facts they have learned about space or flowers, and write it on a chart. The students will include at least one of these sentences in a letter and anything else they want to add. We'll hand out the paper and craft materials and assist the children when necessary.

Outcomes

We expect to bring smiles and laughter to soldiers who have been away from their homes and families defending our country. We want them to know that we appreciate everything they have done for us and are continuing to do for us. This will also create awareness for those children who might not know the severity of what our nation is going through.

End Product

We expect to receive some kind of notification letting us know that the letters were received. We are hoping for some type of response from the soldiers we are writing to. If we do get responses, we will read them to the children and ask them to tell us how they feel about receiving letters from troops in Iraq.

Sample Lesson Plan

Cards for Children in the Hospital

Project Name: Get Well Cards

Grades: K and 1

Teacher: Krishna B.

Type of Service: Indirect

Purpose

By presenting young patients with a card, it will give them a smile and let them know that they are in someone's thoughts.

Need

Children are separated from their families when they are in the hospital. This project is intended to help lift the spirits of children who are either sick or injured in a local hospital by sharing information the students learned about plants and decorating cards with plants and flowers. It also allows the students to think of someone other than themselves.

Standards

Common Core State Standards

English Language Arts: Reading for Information; Key Ideas and Details

English Language Arts: Writing; Text Types and Purpose

Resources and Materials:

- construction paper
- markers

National Science Standards

Life Science: The Characteristics of Organisms

National Curriculum Standards for Social Studies

Civic Ideals and Practices

Student Academic Objectives

- Illustrate a card for a hospitalized child with drawings of plants and flowers.
- Write a fact the student learned about plants.

Student Social Objectives

As the students are making something for someone else, they will explore the concept of giving versus receiving.

Planning and Action

- **Students:** Students will create a card for a child in the hospital.
- **Teacher:** I will provide the materials and discuss the benefits of the activity with the students. I will also deliver the cards.

Outcomes

The students will learn numerous facts about plants. They will also learn to think of others.

End Product

If the student can correctly write a plant fact, then he or she has taken something from the unit. Also, if the student feels good about what she or he has done for another child, the activity will have been a worthwhile experience.

3

Letters to Government Officials

Project Name: Please, Mr. Governor, Save the Rainforest!

Grades: 2 and 3

Teacher: Kari L.

Type of Service: Advocacy

Purpose

This plan is designed to help the children realize the importance of the rainforest. It is intended to get them to care enough to take action to try to save the rainforest. It might also inspire the governor to recognize that this is a real problem that the people in his state care about.

Need

Every day our natural resources are being destroyed. The rainforests are being cut down at such a rate that they may vanish before these students are even old enough to vote. We need to take action to try to get someone here in the United States to care about what is going on around the world, especially in Brazil. The annihilation of the rainforest does not just affect the people living in or near it, but it affects us, too. If the rainforests are destroyed, there will be less oxygen, the earth's climate will change even more, the polar ice caps could melt, and the oceans will rise.

Standards

Common Core State Standards

English Language Arts: Reading for Information; Integration of Knowledge and Ideas

English Language Arts: Writing; Text Types and Purposes

National Curriculum Standards for Social Studies

Global Connections

Student Academic Objectives

Write two effects of cutting down the rainforests in order to persuade the governor to take action and to change policy.

Student Social Objectives

Students will learn about advocacy and the impact of their actions on others.

Resources and Materials:

- postcards or cut cardstock
- crayons, markers, and/or colored pencils
- pencils
- envelope
- postage

Planning and Action

- **Students:** The students will learn about the rainforest and why it is important. They will learn that the rainforests are being cut down and why we need to stop it. In an attempt to help this situation, they will write postcards to our state's governor.

- **Teacher:** After teaching the unit on the rainforests, their importance, and what is currently happening to them, I will ask students to come up with ideas about what to write and draw on postcards. I will mail the postcards to the governor.

Outcomes

As a result, I hope to make the children feel like they can make a difference. I want them to feel empowered. I expect the children to be more aware of the matters relating to the rainforests, too.

End Product

I will collect the postcards and assess the accuracy of the information. I will also ask the students how the project made them feel and continue to monitor rainforest policies and news.

Sample Lesson Plan

Letters and Support for Hurricane Victims

Project Name: Helping Hurricane Victims
Grades: PreK–3
Teacher: Kelley M.
Type of Service: Indirect

Purpose

My class will work to raise money for the hurricane relief fund in our state, which will help communities rebuild their cities and homes. We will also write letters of encouragement to go along with our monetary contributions, so that people will know that others are thinking about them and trying to help. This will hopefully bring a little cheer to people who have been through much devastation recently.

Need

This project is needed because there have been so many disastrous hurricanes in our area recently and students should be aware of this and offer help to families and communities.

Resources and Materials:

- book about hurricanes
- construction paper
- markers/pencils/crayons
- stickers (optional)
- envelopes and stamps
- donations from students, families, and the community
- National Hurricane Center (nhc.noaa.gov)

Standards

Head Start Framework
Literacy: Early Writing; Drawing

Science: Scientific Knowledge

Florida PreK Performance Standards
Language, Communication, and Emergent Literacy: Emergent Reading: Demonstrates comprehension of text read aloud

Language, Communication, and Emergent Literacy: Emergent Writing: Uses scribbling, letter-like shapes, and letters that are clearly different from drawing to represent thoughts and ideas; Demonstrates knowledge of purposes, functions, and structure of written composition

Common Core State Standards
English Language Arts: Reading for Information; Key Ideals and Details

English Language Arts: Writing; Production and Distribution

National Science Standards
Earth Science: Changes in Earth and Sky

Science in Personal and Social Perspectives: Changes in Environments

Student Academic Objectives

Grade PreK

Children will identify that hurricanes are disasters that can affect them. They will draw pictures and copy or dictate words for their letters of support to hurricane victims.

Grades K and 1

Children will identify common characteristics of hurricanes and discuss the effects of hurricanes on families. They will use invented (grade K) or conventional (grade 1) writing skills to write a letter of support for hurricane victims.

Grades 2 and 3

Using information from the National Hurricane Center (nhc.noaa.gov), students will investigate characteristics of hurricanes including types, levels, patterns, locations, and tracking systems. They will also explore the effects of hurricanes on the economy, families, and crops. After discussing the devastation of hurricanes, the students will write letters of encouragement to hurricane victims using correct paragraph structure.

Student Social Objectives

After learning about hurricanes and the devastation that they can cause, children will work together to help each other with their writing. This project will also teach children that they can help others no matter how near or far away they are, and that they don't even have to know someone to be able to help them. Hopefully, they will be inspired to lend a hand to their friends and families.

Planning and Action

We will begin the project by reading a book about hurricanes and learning about natural disasters that are relevant to our area. The students will use listening skills effectively. By writing letters of encouragement to families, the children will be able to communicate their ideas and experiences and will use different types and styles of words to make their messages meaningful to the recipients.

- **Students:** The students in the class will work together to raise money to donate to the hurricane relief fund. They will write letters of encouragement to send to hurricane victims.

- **Teachers:** Other teachers will also tell their classes about our project and help collect money from their students.

Outcomes

We will donate the money and letters to a hurricane relief fund that will give them to families and individuals who have suffered from recent hurricanes. We expect that our letters will be received and will make even a little difference in people's lives. We hope that our contribution will make a difference.

End Product

The product for each grade level will be assessed based on the grade-level objectives.

Student Evaluations

1. Tell me about the project.

- "We collected money to help people because of the hurricane."

- "A lot of people's homes are gone because of hurricanes, so we all brought in money to send to them."

- "We read books about hurricanes and we sent pictures to people."

2. What did you learn from this project that you didn't know before?

- "I learned that hurricanes can ruin houses and buildings."

- "That hurricanes have very strong winds that can blow down trees."

- "I learned that you can help people by giving money and making pictures because it will make people happy."

3. How was your project helpful?

- "It helped people."

- "It made people and families happy."

- "Now we know about hurricanes and that they have strong winds."

4. How did your project help other people/animals/the environment?

- "Because we gave money to people who needed it."

- "We drew pictures to make people happy, because the hurricane took their houses away and they were sad."

- "Now the city can build houses and buildings again."

5. What other things have you done to be helpful since working on your project?

- "I told my parents about the hurricane and they said they would help."

- "I told my mom and dad to make a hurricane kit in case a hurricane comes to town."

Chapter 10

Gardening Projects

The experience of gardening can be rewarding for young children. Through planting seeds and watching the plants grow into flowers, or producing a crop of vegetables, children develop a sense of wonder and appreciation for nature. When children are gardening they engage in activities that are consistent with the characteristics of quality early childhood education, such as first-hand experiences, active participation, interdisciplinary learning, process development, and problem solving. They also develop positive values and attitudes, and comfort with and love of nature. In addition, when the gardening activity is extended to involve others in the community, children practice civic ideals and develop a sense of respect and concern for others.

In this chapter, the sample lesson plans are for students across grade levels preK through three. For example, the first sample lesson plan, "Growing Flowers for Others," can be adapted for preK, K, or first grade. While the lesson plans have been slightly modified for this text, they are essentially identical to the ones that were designed and subsequently taught by early childhood teachers. If you choose one activity to develop children's sense of wonder and excitement about the natural world, the "Butterfly Garden" lesson plan is a must. This is a truly cooperative activity that can involve children, teachers, and family members. After developing the butterfly garden, one way to extend the service learning project is to have the children make flower pens, per the final lesson plan.

Tried and tested in early childhood classrooms, the lesson plans include the relevant standards, instructional objectives, materials needed, and a summary of the activities. The responses of the students who engaged in these activities are captured in the sample student evaluation section.

Sample Lesson Plan

Growing Flowers for Others

Project Name: Flowers for Mom and Sunshine in a Pot
Grades: PreK, K, and 1
Teachers: Ashley S. and Dawn M.
Type of Service: Direct

Purpose

- **Flowers for Mom:** Giving mothers (including stepmothers, guardians, and foster parents) a flower grown by their child brightens their days. Discussing different types of families also promotes tolerance and is part of an anti-bias curriculum. The project gives the children an opportunity to physically see what they have been learning about in their plant unit.

- **Sunshine in a Pot:** Students will witness the growth cycle of a plant's life. They will also learn about the local hospital and why people have to stay longer than one day. This project will hopefully put a smile on a patient's face.

Need

- **Flowers for Mom:** Mother's Day is approaching and the purpose is to have children reflect on the ways that their mothers help them. This will also be a time for us to discuss different types of families. If children have more than one mother figure in their lives (mom, stepmother, etc.), then they should grow a plant for each one.

- **Sunshine in a Pot:** This project may cheer up the spirits of people who are either sick or injured in a local hospital. By giving these patients a potted plant, it will bring the outside in, reminding them that it's springtime, a time of growth and renewal. It may also give patients the extra push they need to get well.

Resources and Materials:

Flowers for Mom
- something to plant the seeds in (we used old dry laundry detergent scoops)
- milk lids (to make wheel barrels out of scoops)
- soil
- marigold seeds
- watering can
- shovels
- construction paper and materials for making cards

Sunshine in a Pot
- starter container for planting seeds
- 1 planting pot per student
- soil
- flower seeds
- hand shovels
- paint, clay, and other art materials
- paintbrushes
- paint sealer

Standards

Head Start Framework

Science: Scientific Knowledge

Literacy: Early Writing; Drawing

Florida PreK Performance Standards

Language, Communication, and Emergent Literacy: Emergent Writing: Shows motivation to engage in written expression

Cognitive Development: Scientific Inquiry: Life Science: Identifies the characteristics of living things

Common Core State Standards

Language Arts: Writing; Text Types and Purposes

National Science Standards

Life Science: Characteristics of Organisms

Student Academic Objectives

Students will:

- identify parts of a plant.
- list the things that a plant needs to grow.

Flowers for Mom

Identify and discuss different types of families.

- **Grade PreK:** Children draw a picture on the card showing one way their moms help them and dictate an accompanying sentence to the teacher.
- **Grades K and 1:** Students draw a picture on the card showing one way their moms help them and write a sentence using invented spelling that corresponds with the picture (grade K) or write two to three sentences using conventional spelling and sentence structure (grade 1).

Sunshine in a Pot

- **Grade PreK:** Children identify art media used to create and paint a pot.

- **Grades K and 1:** Students identify art media used to create and paint a pot. Create/draw a plan for their pot and indicate where they will use at least two types of materials or mediums to decorate the pot.

Student Social Objectives

As the students are making something for someone else, they will be exploring the concept of giving versus receiving.

Planning and Action

Students: Students will plant the seeds and water and care for their plants.

- *Flowers for Mom:* They will then present a grown plant to their mothers for Mother's Day with a card describing one way their moms help them.

- *Sunshine in a Pot:* Students will paint the pots, and plant a small flower for someone who is either sick or injured in the local hospital.

Teachers: We will assist students in planting and ask questions about plant parts and plant life cycles.

- *Flowers for Mom:* We'll lead discussions about different types of families. We will confront child bias and stereotypes about family structures. We will assist students in identifying and writing ways their moms help them.

- *Sunshine in a Pot:* We will assist students in planting; ask questions to reinforce plant parts and life cycles; discuss various art mediums and how they can be used to deco rate pots; and provide all necessary materials. We will coordinate the delivery of the pots to the hospital. If possible, the children will take their plants to the hospital (direct service), or we can deliver the plants and share the patients' responses with students afterward (indirect service). Finally, we will discuss the benefits of this activity with the class.

Outcomes

We expect the children to increase their knowledge of plant parts and the plant life cycle. We also want them to feel proud of what they have accomplished and learn the gift of giving and helping others who are in need.

- **Flowers for Mom:** Students will learn about different types of families.
- **Sunshine in a Pot:** Students will learn about and use a variety of art mediums.

End Product

Through the growth process, we will discuss what changes are taking place in the plant.

- **Flowers for Mom:** During share time, we will discuss how giving mothers the plants will affect them. Students will share how their mothers help them in different ways. Students will tell us how their mothers reacted to receiving the flower.
- **Sunshine in a Pot:** Students will compare the pot plan with the actual product. Discuss with the children the various plans and ways children used the mediums on their pots.

Teacher Evaluation of "Sunshine in a Pot"

The students seemed to really enjoy this service learning project. Before we began the activity, I explained to the students that we would be helping others by spreading a little sunshine through the gift of a potted flower. We discussed the local hospital and the reasons why people had to stay there: sickness, injuries, cancer, pregnancy, etc. We also talked about how sad it can be at the hospital because you aren't at home with your family and usually you aren't feeling well. The students were able to participate in the conversation and many discussed situations where their own family members had been in the hospital.

After our lengthy discussion, I told the students that they would be painting a pot and planting a flower in it for someone in the hospital who was ill or injured. The students asked if they would be taking the pots to the hospital themselves, and I explained that I would be taking the pots there after school. I asked the students, "Do you think the patients will like getting a gift like this in the hospital?" All the students said yes, and one student said, "We sent flowers to my grandmother when she was in the hospital, and she liked them."

The students seemed very interested in the activity and everyone did a wonderful job painting their pots very colorfully. After they dried, I sprayed them with a sealer, and once that dried, the students were able to plant the flower. We planted pretty purple flowers called Hawaii Blues. The activity took the entire day to complete because we worked in small groups. They painted the pots in the morning and planted the flowers in the afternoon. I was very surprised that no one asked to take theirs home; this showed they understood the reason for the activity, which was helping others.

Student Evaluations of "Sunshine in a Pot"

1. Tell me about the "Sunshine in a Pot" project.

- "We painted flower pots and planted a pretty flower in them."
- "Ms. M. is going to take them to the hospital for the people who are sick."
- "When you are sick, presents make you feel better."
- "We sent my grandmother flowers when she was in the hospital, and they made her feel better."

2. What did you learn from this project that you didn't know before?

- "That we need to be nice to people who are sick."
- "Giving someone a present can make them feel better."

3. How was your project helpful?

- "We made people feel better by giving them the pot and flower."
- "It made sick people smile, because someone cared about them."

4. How did your project help other people/animals/the environment?

- "It helped the sick people in the hospital."

5. What other things have you done to be helpful since working on your project?

- "We made cards for them, too."
- "My card said, 'Happy Spring and Get Well Soon.'"

6. How did working on the "Sunshine in a Pot" activity compare to the rest of your schoolwork?

- "It was fun because we got to paint a pot and plant a flower."
- "We had fun making a present for someone who is sick."

3

Beautifying Our School

Project Name: Beautifying Our School
Grades: PreK–3
Teacher: Mimi O.
Type of Service: Direct

Purpose

This project will directly benefit the students and faculty of our elementary school. The location for planting the flowers is a popular spot where students and faculty will be able to see and enjoy them. The students working on this project should feel a sense of pride for helping beautify their school grounds. The goal of this project is for the students to see that they can play a role in giving back to their community.

Need

The area chosen to plant the flowers is not very well kept. It looks like a dirt and weed patch. Since most of our students pass by this area often, we'd like this area to be better maintained. By working on this project, my class will be helping the

Resources and Materials:

- flowers
- shovels
- watering cans
- soil
- gardening gloves
- parent letters explaining the project and asking for help
- digital camera
- donations from a local home improvement store

school while utilizing the knowledge they have just learned in their plant unit.

Standards

Head Start Framework
Science: Scientific Knowledge

Florida PreK Performance Standards
Cognitive Development: Scientific Inquiry: Life Science: Explores growth and change of living things

Common Core State Standards
Mathematics: Measurement and Data: Represent and interpret data

National Science Standards
Life Science: Organisms and Environments

Student Academic Objectives

Grades PreK–3

Students will:

- identify native Florida plants, specifically wild flowers, and discuss why these flowers grow well in this climate.
- identify areas in need of beautification on their school grounds, participate in the planting process, and work to maintain the garden area for the rest of the school year.

Grades 2 and 3

Working in groups, students will observe and track the traffic patterns (before school, during lunch and outside play, after school) for the identified areas of need on the school grounds. Each group will collect data to share with the class so they can make a decision about which area to target for beautification.

Student Social Objectives

Students will:

- work cooperatively with one another by communicating, encouraging, and listening to each other to obtain the goal of this service learning project.

- learn how they can give back to their school community by identifying a school location that is in need of help.

Planning and Action

My plant unit will be preparation for the students to learn how to grow and maintain plants. Specifically, I have a picture splash planned in which students will be cooperatively keeping track of what they know about plants and what they have learned about plants during the week. I will send the students home with a letter asking for flowers and gardening supplies to be donated for this project. Throughout the week, I will organize and collect supplies so at the end of the week on Friday, we will be able to do the project.

- **Students:** All of the students will be responsible for working together to help weed the garden, dig holes, and plant and water their flowers. They will also be responsible for making sure they utilize their learned knowledge to successfully complete this project.

- **Teacher:** I will be responsible for supervising the students and helping them if needed. I will also make sure that all of the supplies are brought together, through donations from others if needed. Lastly, I will start a discussion with the students to make sure they understand what the objectives of this project are and why they are doing it.

- **Community Partners and Other Adults:** A local home improvement store is donating flowers and materials to the school for this project.

Reflection

Students will participate in a class discussion on how they felt about helping their school community. I will ask them why they did this project and what they have learned by doing it. I will review with the students what they have learned about planting flowers and ask them if they were able to use those skills to help plant the flower garden.

Outcomes

I expect that the students will walk away from this service learning project with a new sense of accomplishment through helping their school community. They will learn about how plants grow and what supplies are needed to help. I also expect students to learn that when they work cooperatively together, they can accomplish so much more. Working together will also help strengthen the classroom unity and bonds.

End Product

The students will be evaluated on how effectively they work together through my observational checklist. I will be looking to see if the students were able to correctly plant their flowers, work cooperatively together, and participate in the class discussion following the project.

Documentation

The students' efforts will be documented throughout the project by the photos I will be taking. With the exception of the students whose parents would not let them be photographed, I will upload these photos online to the school's website. This way, students, faculty, and families will be able to see what our class has contributed to the school community.

Celebration

This project is the conclusion of our plant unit, so the class will be celebrating by making "dirt pudding" as part of their unit cooking lesson to enjoy as a fun little snack. The students will also celebrate by completing their picture splash bulletin board displaying all of what they did and learned during their plant unit. The true reward for the students will be their sense of accomplishment they feel every time they pass by the flower garden at school.

Sample Lesson Plan

Butterfly Garden

Project Name: Butterfly Garden
Grades: K and 1
Teacher: Marla J.
Type of Service: Direct

Purpose

Hopefully, the garden will attract butterflies soon after we plant the flowers and plants, which will be a great way for the students to observe butterflies in their natural habitat.

Need

This project is needed because it goes hand in hand with the unit we will be learning. Students will get a chance to beautify the school while doing hands-on activities that teach them about butterflies, specifically plants that attract butterflies.

Standards

National Science Standards
Life Science: Organisms and Environments

Resources and Materials:

- gardening tools—shovels, rulers, watering can, fertilizer
- seeds and flowering plants that attract butterflies; a local home improvement store has offered to contribute seeds and plants
- garden sign to identify the butterfly garden and our class

Student Academic Objectives

Students will:

- identify plants and flowers that attract butterflies.
- list the things a plant needs to grow.
- observe the butterfly garden and weed, water, and feed plants as needed.

Student Social Objectives

The students will be put in groups of four (called "butterfly buddies"). They will be assigned different tasks to study butterfly plants and do the planting. Cooperative learning is a key factor in this project, as well as being able to pay close attention and follow instructions.

Planning and Action

- **Students:** All of the students in the class will participate in their butterfly buddy groups to plant seeds, flowers, and plants that attract butterflies.
- **Teachers:** I will oversee the students' work.

Outcomes

Students will learn about plants, how to grow flowers, and what plants need in order to create a great garden. They will observe and tend the garden daily to keep it clean and pretty, so it will attract butterflies.

End Product

I will take photos of the students planting and working in the garden. Photos will continue to be taken every week on the same day so we can see how the plants are growing.

Sample Lesson Plan

Flower Pens

Project Name: Saying Thank You with Flowers
Grades: PreK–3
Teacher: Ashley R.
Type of Service: Direct

Purpose

This project will help the school community by showing all staff that children are grateful for what they do. It will teach the children that the school runs because of every single person who works there. It will also teach them to all work together and be thankful for one another.

Need

This project is needed to show the children to be thankful for everyone who works at their school, because without them the school would not be open or run smoothly. It will be integrated into the curriculum as the children are learning about plants, and they will make flower pens for the staff. Writing and drawing will also be integrated into this project as the students write thank-you cards to give to the staff along with the pens.

Resources and Materials:

- green tape
- pens
- a variety of silk flowers with a stem, or material to construct various flowers
- construction paper
- markers
- crayons
- pencils
- camera

Standards

Head Start Framework
Science: Scientific Knowledge

Literacy: Early Writing

Florida PreK Performance Standards
Language, Communication, and Emergent Literacy: Emergent Writing: Uses scribbling, letter-like shapes, and letters that are clearly different from drawing to represent thoughts and ideas; Demonstrates knowledge of purposes, functions, and structure of written composition

Cognitive Development: Scientific Inquiry: Life Science: Identifies characteristics of living things

National Curriculum Standards for Social Studies
Civic Ideals and Practices

Common Core State Standards
English Language Arts: Writing; Text Types and Purposes

National Science Standards
Life Science: Characteristics of Organisms

Student Academic Objectives

Grades PreK–3
Students will apply elements of being a good citizen in their school community (social studies) and they will create a visual representation of a flower (science). This project will also cover language arts when they write or draw thank-you cards for the staff.

Grades 2 and 3

Students will identify characteristics of responsible citizens in the various school staff positions. They will create flow charts to demonstrate the impact of staff members' jobs on students.

Student Social Objectives

Students will identify what it means to have good character and be a good school citizen, as well as practice good social skills. They will be learning how to say "thank you" and show appreciation for others.

Planning and Action

- **Students:** After studying different flowers, the students will make flower pens and thank-you cards for the school staff. Then they will personally hand the pen and card that they made to one of the staff members.
- **Teacher:** Before the project begins, I will get the staff members' names and discuss the service learning project with them. I will talk with students about elements of good character and citizenship. Discussion will also include why thanking others is so important and how they're making a difference. I will plan a time to take small groups of children out of class to hand out their pens and cards to staff members.
- **Community Partners and Other Adults:** The staff at the school will meet with students to discuss their jobs and help explain how their jobs impact the students. Second- and third-grade students will shadow various staff members to document the impact of their positions on students and adults in their school.

Reflection

Grades PreK–3

After the students make the card and pen, they will share with the teacher why they think what they are doing is important and how their pen reflects the flower that they chose to make. Then, after passing out the cards and pens, students will share what happened when they gave their gift and how it made them feel. Finally, class members will

discuss why this project was important and how it helped make them good citizens.

Grades 2 and 3

Based on what they learned during shadowing, students will predict what would happen to the school if particular staff members didn't show up for work.

End Product

Grades PreK–3

Each flower pen should resemble the specific flower chosen by the child. This match will demonstrate observation and knowledge of the flower. As the cards are being made, I will evaluate if the students drew or wrote characteristics of being a good citizen. I will take photos of all the cards and flower pens the students made. I will also photograph the children passing out their cards and pens to staff members. This will show them being a good citizen and it will show the staff's appreciation.

Grades PreK and K

During the final reflection, I will write down what the children say they have learned and experienced from the project and make two posters. One poster will hang in the classroom, and one will hang in the library, lunchroom, or school office.

Grades 1, 2, and 3

During the final reflection, the students will write what they have learned and experienced from the project and make two posters. One poster will hang in the classroom, and one will hang in the library, lunchroom, or school office.

Documentation

The learning gained from this project will be shared through the classroom poster and the poster that is hung in another place in the school.

Celebration

The project and learning experience will be celebrated by having a cupcake party at the end of the week. As a class, we will celebrate being good citizens.

Helping Others

The sample lesson plans in this chapter were designed by teachers as part of their service learning projects focused on the goal of helping others. The first sample lesson plan is an ideal activity for those weeks leading up to the Thanksgiving holiday. The teachers who taught this lesson agreed that the project was a welcome change from the traditional, and often stereotypical, Thanksgiving lessons. With remarks from the students such as "Some people don't get turkey on Thanksgiving," it was evident that children's learning extended beyond traditional academic subjects.

Helping those in need is the direct concern of the second sample lesson plan. This is an excellent example of indirect service with kindergarten or first-grade students. While learning the mathematical skills of measuring, data collection, and classifying, young children also do something for the greater good. While the focus is on helping others,

the content standards specified in the plan ensure that academic learning is not neglected.

In the third project, children learn the simple yet important reality that everyone needs a place to live. This is an activity that can be easily adapted for any of the early childhood grades. As an example of direct service, it clearly integrates many aspects of the curriculum. It's a perfect example of authentic and experiential learning that extends beyond "hands on and minds on" by enabling children to actually *do* something about their concern for others.

Thinking about others is also the focus of the final sample lesson plan in this chapter. It's a wonderful way for children to reflect on their random acts of kindness, while at the same time practicing and developing their writing skills. This lesson illustrates how the simplest of activities requiring very few materials and resources can be transformed into a service learning project. The activities provide the perfect motivation for students to write, and the suggested celebration event helps to involve parents in their children's learning.

Sample Lesson Plan

Second Harvest

Project Name: Second Harvest
Grades: PreK–3
Teachers: Lauren and April
Type of Service: Indirect

Purpose

We will donate food and placemats to the local Second Harvest. Second Harvest collects food and distributes it to nonprofit organizations in the community. These organizations then give the food to families in need. We plan to have a representative from Second Harvest come to the school to discuss the organization and how it helps people in the community.

Need

The first Thanksgiving was celebrated in 1621 by the Pilgrims of the Plymouth Colony and about 90 Wampanoag Native Americans. The Pilgrims had suffered through a devastating winter in which nearly half of them died. Without the help of the Native Americans, all would have perished. As a class, we are going to help others by collecting canned goods and other nonperishable food items for the local Second Harvest. We are also going to make fall-themed placemats for the families who receive the food from Second Harvest.

Standards

Head Start Framework
Mathematics: Patterns and Measurements

Creative Arts: Art

Florida PreK Performance Standards
Cognitive Development: Mathematical Thinking: Patterns and Seriation: Sorts, orders, compares, and describes objects according to characteristics or attributes

Cognitive Development: Mathematical Thinking: Measurement: Represents and analyzes data

Common Core State Standards
Mathematics: Measurement and Data

National Curriculum Standards for Social Studies
Civic Ideals and Practices

National Standards for Visual Arts
Content Standard #1: Applying Media

Student Academic Objectives

Grades PreK–3
Students will:

- make food collection bins, posters, and flyers to place around the school.

- bring in and collect canned goods and other nonperishable food items.

Resources and Materials:

- local Second Harvest contact information and representative to come to the school
- collection bins and boxes
- construction paper
- markers, crayons, paints
- posters
- flyers
- placemats
- class or individual graph

- make fall-themed placemats.
- identify at least one thing that they are thankful for and one to three ways they can help others in their community.
- graph collected items (PreK and K will do this as a class; Grades 1, 2, and 3 will do this in small groups).

Grades 2 and 3

Compare and contrast the graph of collected items to the food needs of individuals and families, and identify items from the food pyramid that are still needed so all people can have a more nutritious meal.

Student Social Objectives

Students will focus on helping behaviors by working with others in the class and by giving food.

Planning and Action

- **Students:** They will make food collection bins, posters, and flyers to place around the school, and collect canned goods and other nonperishable food items. They will also make fall-themed placemats.
- **Teachers:** We will facilitate the project and deliver the food and placemats to the local Second Harvest.
- **Community Partners and Other Adults:** The local Second Harvest will distribute the food to nonprofit organizations that provide food to people in need.

Outcomes

At the end of this project, we want our students to have a better understanding of the needs of people in their community, realize how much they have to be thankful for, feel good about helping others, and identify more ways they can be helpful.

End Product

We will use a checklist to make sure that every child is helping with the collection bins, posters, and flyers; has completed a placement; and has contributed to or completed a graph of the items collected.

Teacher Evaluation

This project was not difficult for our students. It had an impact on them because young children can be very egocentric and they often don't think about others who are less fortunate than they are. This project helped them think about others and reflect on the things they have in their lives. This differed from our usual lessons because it was ongoing; every day, children brought in canned goods and at the end of the day we added the information to the graph. It was also different because we usually have a strong focus on language arts, but this was a social studies lesson that involved teaching about others and being generous to other people. The students were engaged because they wanted to have a lot of food to donate to those in need.

When we made placemats to give along with the food, students took special care in the paintings they made and in writing *Happy Thanksgiving*. They were saying things like "I want to make sure I spell it correctly," and "I hope they think this is pretty." We used our usual classroom management strategies, and children had free choice as to what type of art medium they wanted to use to make their placemats. They were all excited to do it.

Student Evaluations

1. Why do you like helping people?
- "It makes them happy."
- "Because they are my friends."
- "Because when they say 'thank you,' I feel special."
- "Because I like to share."

2. Why is it helpful to help others?
- "They can get better."
- "So they aren't hungry."
- "In case they are hurt, you can try to help."
- "To make them feel better."

3. What did you learn from the project?
- "That some people don't get to eat like we do."
- "To give to people who need it."
- "Some people don't get turkey on Thanksgiving."
- "That we helped people."

4. What else could you do to help others?
- "Give presents for Christmas."
- "Help with hard work in class."
- "Help them do their math."
- "Clean up [play] centers even when I didn't play there."

Helping Those in Need

Project Name: Helping Those in Need
Grades: K and 1
Teacher: Lisa
Type of Service: Indirect

Purpose

Students will learn about adults and children in their community who do not have enough food or clothes. We will discuss how we can share what we have with others in need and the kids will bring in some of their own food, clothes, and toys to give to other people in the community who really need them.

Resources and Materials:

- letter to parents explaining project and how to work with their child in selecting items to donate
- *The Lady in the Box* by Ann McGovern
- *Think of Those in Need* by Stan and Jan Berenstain
- journals, pencils, and crayons
- class, group, or individual graphs
- community partners and other people to come to the school to talk about how they help others
- transportation to drop off donated items

Need

This project is needed because many people in the community do not have enough food to eat, clothes to wear, or other items.

Standards

Common Core State Standards

Mathematics: Measurement and Data

English Language Arts: Writing; Text Types and Purposes

National Curriculum Standards for Social Studies

Individuals, Groups, and Institutions: Civic Ideals and Practices

Student Academic Objectives

Students will:

- identify local organizations that help people in need (Red Cross, Homeless Shelter, Good Will) and discuss the ways these organization help them.

- work with their parents to sort through their clothes, toys, and food, and identify items they no longer need that they can donate to people who might need them.

- graph by category the items brought in.

- write in journals about the different organizations and ways they are helping others; the process of sorting their items at home and how they made their decisions; ways they could help others in their community; and how they feel after donating their items.

Student Social Objectives

- Giving
- Helping others
- Being thankful

Planning and Action

- **Students:** They will learn about people in need in the community; graph items brought in; bring in food, clothes, and toys; and reflect in their journals about how can they can help other people and why it is important.

- **Teacher:** I will read *The Lady in the Box* by Ann McGovern and *Think of Those in Need* by Stan and Jan Berenstain. I'll explain to students what the project will be about, using examples from the two books. I will also bring donated items to the final destination.

- **Community Partners and Other Adults:** The local homeless shelter will be receiving the food donations we collect. The Red Cross will receive the other donated items.

Outcomes

The students will understand that people in their community have different amounts of goods, learn the importance of helping others, and be thankful for what they have. Students will write about this in their journals.

End Product

We will have the graphs of the items the students collected and their journal writings.

Sample Lesson Plan

Habitats for Habitat for Humanity

Project Name: Habitat for Humanity—Helping in Our Habitat!

Grades: PreK–3

Teacher: Tori C.

Type of Service: Direct

Purpose

This project will help others in the community by providing them with birdhouses created by my students for their new homes.

Need

The unit taught during this project will be "Habitats and Food Chains." Students will learn about habitats around the world, their own habitat in the community, and habitats for birds. This project will also focus on helping others in the community who have faced disaster and need help rebuilding their homes. The students will learn about helping the less fortunate in their community by creating birdhouses for their homes.

Standards

Head Start Framework

Science: Scientific Knowledge

Literacy: Early Writing

Social and Emotional Development: Knowledge of Families and Communities

Florida PreK Performance Standards

Social and Emotional Development: Relationships: Shows care and concern for others

Language, Communication, and Emergent Literacy: Emergent Writing: Uses scribbling, letter-like shapes, and letters that are clearly different from drawing to represent thoughts and ideas

Cognitive Development: Scientific Inquiry: Earth and Space: Explores outdoor environment and begins to recognize changes in the environment

Cognitive Development: Scientific Inquiry: Environmental Awareness: Demonstrates ongoing environmental awareness and responsibility with teacher support and multiple experiences over time

Common Core State Standards

Mathematics: Measurement and Data

Resources and Materials:

- materials for constructing birdhouses or precut wooden birdhouses for each group
- outdoor tempura paint in varying colors
- camera
- journals
- graphic organizers
- representative from Habitat for Humanity
- *Dewey Doo-It Builds a House: A Children's Story About Habitat for Humanity* by Brahm Wenger and Alan Green

National Science Standards

Life Science: Organisms and Environments

Science in Personal and Social Perspectives: Changes in Environment

National Curriculum Standards for Social Studies

People, Places, and Environments: Civic Ideals and Practices

National Standards for Visual Arts

Content Standard #1: Applying Media

Student Academic Objectives

Grade PreK

Students will:

- identify characteristics of their habitat and the habitats of birds. They will identify similarities and differences between their habitats and bird habitats.

- reflect on the process of learning about habitats and planning and building the birdhouses by contributing to the class journal that will record the service learning process.

Grades PreK–3

- Students will identify reasons people need help rebuilding their houses and how Habitat for Humanity helps them.

Grades K and 1

Students will:

- assemble precut birdhouses using wood glue.

- plan and paint the birdhouses to give to families who have had their homes built by Habitat for Humanity.

Grades K–3

Students will:

- compare and contrast habitats around the world with their own habitat in the community and with habitats for birds.

- be able to identify reasons people need help rebuilding their houses and how Habitat for Humanity can help them.

Grades 2 and 3

- After learning how to appropriately use tools from the home improvement store representative (hammers, nails, clamps, pliers, etc.), each student group will plan and assemble their birdhouse under adult supervision using the tools and wood glue.

- When constructed, each group will paint their birdhouse.

- They will give their birdhouse to a family who has had their home built by Habitat for Humanity.

Student Social Objectives

The students will identify characteristics of being a good citizen and the importance of giving back to the community, especially during a recession or after a natural disaster. The students will also learn that they can use their creativity to give back to the community and that it can be fun as well as rewarding.

Planning and Action

- **Students:** The students will learn about Habitat for Humanity initially by reading *Dewey Doo-It Builds a House* in class. The students will create and/or paint one birdhouse in their small groups. Using a graphic organizer, they will plan out how to assemble or build the birdhouse and/or paint each birdhouse and then execute the plans.

- **Teacher:** I will purchase wood for birdhouses or purchase unfinished birdhouses for each group, and will also provide the paint and planning materials. I will contact Habitat for Humanity to request for a person from the organization to come and talk to the class about what they do and who they serve.

- **Community Partners and Other Adults:** A representative from Habitat for Humanity will visit the classroom and provide pictures of previous projects the group has worked on. The representative will explain what Habitat for Humanity is and how they help their community. A local home improvement store will donate the wood, nails, hooks, chains, and/or birdhouses for the project.

Reflection

The students will reflect in their journals on what they have learned about Habitat for Humanity, the people they serve, and how they think the birdhouses they made will help their community.

End Product

The birdhouses will be the final products that are collected from the project.

Documentation

I will document this project by taking photos of the students while they are working on the birdhouses, when they are learning how to use the materials (grades 2 and 3), and while they are participating in the presentation from Habitat for Humanity. I will also document this project by collecting the graphic organizers and journals from my students.

Celebration

To celebrate the project, we will create a board to post in school to display the photos taken of the students so that students, parents, teachers, and other school staff will be able to see these pictures, learn about Habitat for Humanity, and find out ways they can help others in their community.

Sample Lesson Plan

Acts of Kindness

Project Name: Pay It Forward: Measurable Acts of Kindness
Grades: PreK–3
Teacher: Jennifer H.
Type of Service: Direct

Purpose

In this project, parents, staff, and the community will join students in performing random acts of kindness. Every kind act will be recorded on a strip of paper and added to a paper chain on an ongoing basis. This project helps students learn about and build positive character skills. By learning to become better people, students will set a good example for everyone and perhaps motivate community members to join them in their efforts to become kind and thoughtful members of society.

Need

This project is needed to help strengthen and build a strong community of caring citizens. In society today, many children grow up with the mindset

of "every man for himself." Although this mindset is often part of reality, young children should be exposed to the concept of kindness, because it can have a great impact on what type of people they will grow up to be.

Standards

Head Start Framework
Social and Emotional Development: Knowledge of Families and Communities

Literacy: Early Writing

Florida PreK Performance Standards
Language, Communication, and Emergent Literacy: Emergent Writing: Uses scribbling, letter-like shapes, and letters that are clearly different from drawing to represent thoughts and ideas

Social and Emotional Development: Relationships: Shows care and concern for others

Common Core State Standards
Mathematics: Measurement and Data

English Language Arts: Writing; Text Types and Purposes

National Curriculum Standards for Social Studies
Civic Ideals and Practices

Student Academic Objectives

Students will:

- identify characteristics of being a good citizen through kind acts or ways to "pay it forward."
- identify, record, graph, and measure acts of kindness.

Resources and Materials:

- strips of paper
- tape or a stapler
- markers, crayons, pencils
- video clip from the movie *Pay It Forward*
- materials to make "Kindness Zone" posters
- letter to parents
- poster paper for graph

Grade PreK

Students will:

- draw the act of kindness on the strips of paper.
- record their reflections on the project in their journals.
- count and measure the strips and participate in the class graph discussion.

Grades K and 1

Students will:

- draw and/or write key words to describe the act of kindness on the strips of paper. In their journals, they will draw and use invented and conventional spelling to reflect on the project.
- use counting strategies, measure the strips, and add to the class graph or create their own graph.

Grades 2 and 3

Students will:

- write one to three sentences to describe the act of kindness on the strips of paper. In their journals, they will write five or more sentences to describe the act of kindness and reflect on the data in the graph.
- use counting strategies, place-value strategies, and addition skills as they keep a running total of chains for their classroom and other participating classrooms.

Student Social Objectives

Students will:

- identify acts of kindness and learn how to be a kind person.
- practice acts of kindness and reflect on how it makes them feel and discuss reactions when they see or perform acts of kindness.

Planning and Action

- **Students:** Students will be introduced to the project through a discussion of what it means to be kind. They may watch a clip of the movie *Pay It Forward*. The class will role-play

behaviors and the students will decide if the behavior is an act of kindness or not. Students will practice acting out a kind act with each other. Finally, students will learn about the kindness chain and will begin recording the kind acts they see or do on strips of paper. Throughout the day, students can add to the chain or nominate someone who has performed an act of kindness to add to the chain. Acts of kindness will be measured and graphed at the end of each day or week. During the project, students will recite the Golden Rule every morning. Students will also create "Kindness Zone" posters to be displayed in the school.

- **Teacher:** I will integrate this project into the existing curriculum on a daily basis and will join my class in the project. I will also ask other teachers if they want to participate. If they do, my students will go to their classroom to discuss the project and tell them what to do. Following, they will be provided with details about the project, materials needed to participate, and letters to send home to parents.

- **Community Partners and Other Adults:** Parents will be notified of this project before it starts and will be asked to "pay it forward" at home to provide students with consistency and to model the pattern of kind acts. School staff will be notified of the project in the school's monthly newsletter and encouraged to participate. Other adults will be informed of the project through letters asking for support.

Reflection

Students will have an opportunity to reflect on the project during daily journal time. They will be asked to write and draw about the kindness project at the end of the week.

Outcomes

The success of the project will be evident as the paper chain grows and the graphing results get bigger. Students will talk about acts of kindness and performing acts of kindness on a more regular basis.

End Products

Throughout the project, on a weekly basis, the teacher will collect the kindness chains from each classroom or students will deliver the kindness chains. Additionally, teachers will read through student journals.

Documentation

At the end of the project, each class chain will be linked to create a large one. The chain will be placed in a circle on a large field or playground and viewed by others at the school.

Celebration

The school will celebrate their success in performing kind acts by having a "Kindness Picnic." Parents will be invited to join their child at the picnic. On the day of the picnic, students will be invited to make a "Kindness Circle" by sitting together inside one of the paper chains.

Chapter 12

Environmental Issues

According to a recent report, engaging children in the natural world includes imparting knowledge about the environment, as well as about emotions, dispositions, and skills.[1] The lesson plans described in this chapter will help children develop an appreciation for the world around them. The teachers have designed simple activities in familiar environments, because they know that children learn best through experiences that relate to what they already know. The best place to start is often in the classroom, school yard, or local park.

In the first lesson, the children experience indirect service by engaging in activities to help keep their school clean. While practicing language and mathematical skills, the children take action that will improve their immediate environment.

This theme is extended in the second sample lesson plan, where children learn about different ways they can recycle. The students' products and actions resulting from this lesson are important, but perhaps more important is the lasting impact on children's attitudes and values.

The final sample lesson plan is designed to teach children about endangered species and how they can take action to make a difference. Children often learn that the threat of extinction for certain animals is due to the actions of others. The animals and related threats are often far removed from their personal experience, so these teachers have designed activities that the children can relate to personally. By taking action, the children gain a deeper understanding of concepts such as conservation, environment, and endangered species. Hopefully, the lessons and activities described in this chapter will extend children's appreciation of nature and the environment, and perhaps develop in them a desire to protect it for the future.

---

[1] Early Childhood Environmental Education (North American Association for Environmental Education, 2010)

Sample Lesson Plan

School Trash and Pollution

Project Name: School Cleanup

Grade Levels: PreK–3

Teachers: Cassie F., Hannah L., Magen D., Christiana A.

Type of Service: Indirect

Purpose

The purpose of this service learning plan is to teach the students the effects of litter, trash, and pollution on the environment. Children will learn the importance of keeping a clean school environment for the safety of their school community.

Need

This project will give the students hands-on experience to learn why it is so important to keep our environment clean for people, as well as for animals, and what we can do as individuals to help. They will learn that if trash is not picked up off the ground it can end up being blown into rivers, lakes, or oceans, and can harm animals and people.

Standards

Head Start Framework

Literacy: Early Writing

Social and Emotional Development: Knowledge of Families and Community

Mathematics: Number and Operations; Patterns and Measurement

Florida PreK Performance Standards

Language, Communication, and Emergent Literacy: Emergent Writing: Shows motivation to engage in written expression

Cognitive Development: Scientific Inquiry: Environmental Awareness: Demonstrates ongoing environmental awareness and responsibility

Mathematical Thinking: Patterns and Seriation: Sorts, orders, compares, and describes objects according to characteristics or attributes

Mathematical Thinking: Measurement: Represents and analyzes data

Common Core State Standards

English Language Arts: Writing; Text Types and Purposes

Mathematics: Measurement and Data; Counting and Cardinality; Operations and Algebraic Thinking

Resources and Materials:

- collection bags for each student
- gloves for each student
- class and/or individual graph paper
- containers of different sizes for estimation activity
- student journals
- guest speaker from local landfill or recycling center

National Science Standards

Science Impersonal and Social Perspectives: Changes in Environment

National Curriculum Standards for Social Studies

People, Places, and Environments

Student Academic Objectives

Students will:

- identify types of pollution.
- discuss harmful effects of pollution on the environment.
- participate in cleaning up the school by collecting trash and putting it in garbage bags.
- estimate and graph how much garbage is collected.
  - **Grade PreK:** Students will estimate by identifying a container when given three sizes of containers; count trash items; and contribute to the class trash graph.
  - **Grades K–1:** Students will estimate, most to least, which trash items discussed will be found as they clean up the school area; identify a container when given five sizes of containers; contribute to class or group trash graph; and compare and contrast their estimations with the actual amount collected.
  - **Grades 2–3:** Students will identify in amount or weight, from most to least, which trash items discussed would be found as they clean up the school area; create an individual trash graph and contribute their data to a class trash graph; compare and contrast their estimations to the actual amount or weight collected.
- draw and/or write in their journals about what they have learned and what they can do to continue to keep the school community clean.
  - **Grade PreK:** Students will draw pictures identifying types of trash, the effect of trash on the environment, and one way they can help stop pollution.
  - **Grades K–1:** Students will draw and write, using invented and/or conventional spelling, the types of trash found, its effect on the environment, and two ways they can help stop pollution.
  - **Grades 2–3:** Students will write and illustrate a story or paragraph about the types of trash found, its immediate and long-term effect on the environment, two ways they can individually help stop pollution, and ways their school can help stop pollution. They will also use class data and project the monthly and yearly amount of trash for their school and estimate its effect on their school environment.

Student Social Objectives

Students will:

- cooperate in groups and/or as a class to clean up the school grounds by collecting trash.
- reflect on being responsible for collecting their own garbage and putting it in a bag and being a community helper to keep a clean school environment for everyone.

Planning and Action

- **Students:** All of the students will be given a bag and a pair of gloves to wear as they walk around the school campus to pick up whatever trash or litter they find on the ground and put it in their bag. When the students get back to the classroom, they will estimate and graph how much trash was found. They will participate in a class discussion about what they did, the benefit of their service, and how they can continue to help keep the environment clean. From this discussion the students will record in their journals what they have learned and how they can continue to help keep the community clean.
- **Teachers:** We will plan a lesson about the dangers of litter and pollution to oceans and the land and will invite a representative from the local landfill or recycling center to talk to the class about trash and where it ends up. We

will pass out trash collection materials to all of the students and will lead the class on a walk around the school. We will then ask students about what they have done and learned, and how they can continue to help the community. As the students are responding to the questions, we may write their responses on the board before giving them their journals to write in. The students can use the sentences on the board as a reference while journaling.

- **Community Partners and Other Adults:** Representative from a local landfill or recycling center will speak to the class.

Reflection

- Before the walk, the class will talk about the areas around the school where they have seen trash so they have input into where they are going to clean up.
- After the walk, the students will reflect on the trash they collected and how much they think others have collected to estimate the total amount of trash the class cleaned up.
- Finally, the students will reflect on the experience as a whole by writing in their journals after the class discussion and/or guest presentation.

Outcomes/End Products

- The trash collected by the class will be used as a visual to show how much they helped the school by cleaning up a few areas.
- The graphs will be collected to see the students' estimations of the trash found.
- The journals will be read afterward to see what the students have learned and how they plan to keep using the skills they have learned.

Documentation

- The class graph or data will be shared with the school administration and other classes.
- The class will share data and what students can do in the school newsletter and on the morning school announcements.
- The class will contact other teachers to see if they are willing to be responsible for trash pickup—maybe one class per month.

Celebration

After the students have written in their journals, there will be a celebration. We will make a "Dirt Dessert" (see recipe below) with gummy worms. We will discuss how cleaning up the schools will help animals and people live better.

Dirt Dessert Recipe

1¼ lbs. Oreo cookies, crushed
3 lg. pkgs. vanilla instant pudding
12 oz. soft cream cheese
6 oz. whipped topping
4½ c. milk
1 flower planter (pot), approximately 10 inches in diameter
1 gummy worm
1 bunch plastic flowers

Directions: Whip together pudding, cream cheese, whipped topping, and milk. Layer flower planter with crushed cookies and pudding mix (be sure crushed cookies are on the bottom first) and save some crushed cookies for the top of your planter. Decorate with worm and flowers. You may want to wrap stem of flowers in a baggy for easier cleaning and reuse. Enjoy!

Sample Lesson Plan

School Recycling

Project Name: We Can Recycle!
Grades: K and 1
Teachers: Alder T. and Anya T.
Type of Service: Direct, Advocacy

Purpose

This project will help others in the community because we will be recycling, which is helpful to our entire environment. It also helps the recipients of the letters students will write, because they will learn about the importance of recycling. Recycling benefits everyone by decreasing pollution and litter.

Need

This plan is needed because children should know the importance of recycling at home and at school. If we don't recycle we can harm our environment.

Standards

Common Core State Standards

English Language Arts: Writing; Text Types and Purposes

Resources and Materials:

- writing paper
- pencils
- crayons
- recycling bin
- chart describing what can be recycled

National Science Standards

Science Impersonal and Social Perspectives: Changes in Environment

Student Academic Objectives

Students will:

- identify types of air pollution and the effect of each on the environment and on humans.
- draw and/or write two ways a child in another class can recycle at home or at school.
- participate in recycling efforts of the classroom.

Student Social Objectives

Students will practice cooperation by working together in groups to draw/write the letter to the teacher and discuss recycling in their class.

Planning and Action

- **Students:** Students will use the recycling bin to collect paper, plastic bottles, and other recyclable items. Once a month, they will empty the bin behind the school. Plastic and metal items will be taken to a recycling center and exchanged for money. The students will also create a letter for a chosen teacher and class to explain to them how recycling can help our world, and encourage them to recycle in their classroom, too.

- **Teachers:** We will teach the kids about recycling to find out what they already know, and provide other important information about recycling and why it is important. We will learn how to start recycling every day in the classroom by sorting trash and reusing paper when possible. We will provide a classroom recycle bin. While students are writing the letters, we will be checking their spelling and sentence structure.

Outcomes

We expect our students to have a better understanding of the importance of recycling, and for them to share what they know with others. We also expect our students to start recycling as much as possible, especially in the classroom.

End Product

Evidence for this project will be seeing if the children recycle more; there will be less paper in the garbage can. We can also ask some of the parents if their children have taken an interest in recycling at home also.

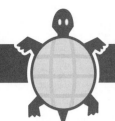

Sample Lesson Plan

Conservation Protects and Saves Animals

Project Name: Save the Animals by Conserving Energy

Grades: PreK–3

Teachers: Lauren, Sheena, Jamie, Breanna, Kelly, Sarah, Indinul, Annie, Leah

Type of Service: Advocacy

Purpose

Although the endangered animals in this project (whales, dolphins, manatees, sea turtles, jaguarondi, koalas, pandas, and elephants) are not part of our school environment, we will learn that our practices have a direct influence on our environment and on them. Therefore, it is important to us to learn how to change our behaviors (save energy, reduce pollution, buy items that don't contain ivory, protest poaching, etc.). We will also help those around us become more aware of these endangered animals so they can also change their actions.

Need

This project is needed because the threats facing these animals are numerous. If we do not work together to eliminate the many threats posed to these animals, these fantastic creatures could become extinct.

Standards

Head Start Framework

Science: Scientific Knowledge

Literacy: Early Writing

Florida PreK Performance Standards

Language, Communication, and Emergent Literacy: Emergent Reading: Demonstrates comprehension of text read aloud; Vocabulary: Shows an understanding of words and their meanings

Cognitive Development: Scientific Inquiry: Earth and Space: Explores outdoor environment and begins to recognize changes in the environment, with teacher and multiple experiences over time; Environmental Awareness: Demonstrates ongoing environmental awareness and responsibility with teacher support and multiple experiences over time

Resources and Materials:

- guest speaker information
- information and pictures regarding endangered animals and what we can do to help
- poster materials:
  - poster board
  - pencils
  - crayons
  - markers
- paper to make cards
- addresses of where we're going to send the cards
- monetary donations for "adopt an animal" program (if relevant)
- books on endangered animals

Common Core State Standards

English Language Arts: Writing; Text Types and Purposes

National Science Standards

Earth Science: Properties of Earth Materials

Science in Personal Perspectives: Changes in Environment

National Curriculum Social Standards for Studies

People, Places, and Environments

Student Academic Objectives

Students will:

- tell or write the difference between endangered and extinct.
- identify practices that are causing the animal to become endangered or extinct.
- draw and/or write behaviors that they can change in order to help the animal.
- write to communicate ideas and information effectively.
- identify the need for protecting the natural systems of earth and explain the interdependent, cyclic nature of living things in the environment.
- identify one or more consequences of using limited natural resources.
- create and communicate a range of subject matter, symbols, and ideas using knowledge of structures and functions of visual arts.

Student Social Objectives

This project will explore and/or teach the behavioral/social skills/concepts of working cooperatively by taking turns, practicing equally, patiently waiting, communicating clearly, following directions, paraphrasing, staying with the team, celebrating success, and helping others.

Planning and Action

- **Students:** Through guest speakers, stories, and research, the students will first learn about the animal, why it is becoming endangered, which foundations or places work to take care of this species, and why it is important to help it. They will take steps to conserve energy, reduce pollution, etc., in their own lives to improve the environment for these animals. Then, they will pass along to others the information they have learned. They will make posters about saving the animal, and/or write cards to foundations and/or government officials.

- **Teachers:** We will organize the guest speaker from a local wildlife foundation to come and speak to the children. We will use stories, websites, and lessons to teach the children about the animal and why it is endangered.

- **Community Partners and Other Adults:** Foundations and organizations will be contacted depending on the animal focus.

Outcomes

First, we expect to help others become more knowledgeable and aware of the importance of saving these animals. We also expect to help others understand that their actions can affect whether these animals survive or become extinct. If we can make others aware, they can join us to help protect these endangered animals. We expect the students to gain an appreciation for endangered species and learn ways that they can help prevent extinction.

End Product

Through the children's drawings and/or writings, we will find out if they have met the project objectives. We will ask other students throughout the school to see if they know about the endangerment of the animal, if they saw our posters, and what they are going to do to help.

Student Evaluations

1. Tell me about this project.

"It was so much fun! We used gray paper to make the trunks and used white paper for the tusks. We did it because we wanted to save the elephants and let everyone know they are in trouble."

2. What did you learn from this project that you didn't know before?

"We learned that elephants are killed for their tusks by hunters to make jewelry and other things. I also learned not to kill elephants."

3. How was your project helpful?

"It was helpful because other students will look at the posters and then they will want to save the elephants. We also don't want the elephants to become extinct."

4. How did your project help other people/animals/the environment?

"It helped so that the elephants can stay alive and so that everyone can help them once they see our posters."

5. What other things have you done to be helpful since working on your project?

"We have told a lot of people about it. Once they know then they can tell people so it will save the elephants."

6. How did working on the project compare to the rest of your schoolwork?

"Making the posters was the best part of everything. I like being able to help others and let everyone know about it."

Teacher Evaluation

1. Tell us about your service learning project.

My unit was on elephants so we did a service learning project about saving the elephants. First we discussed why elephants are in danger. I showed several pictures and explained things we could do to help them. One thing we could do is make posters that say SAVE THE ELEPHANTS and hang them around school to inform everyone about elephants being in danger.

2. Describe any involvement of community members or organizations.

I wrote a letter to a representative from The Elephants of Cameroon. This organization raises money and awareness for elephants. I included some pictures of our class with the posters they made. The representative contacted me and said he put some of the students' work on the organization's website to let all of its visitors know that children of any age can help make a difference.

3. How effective was the service learning project for your class?

The project was very effective. The students really got into it and wanted everyone to know about it. They understood why we were doing the project and how it was helping elephants.

4. How did your students benefit from the service learning project.

The students now have a clear definition of what *extinct* and *endangered* mean, why elephants are becoming extinct and endangered, and how to share their knowledge with others. At first, my students didn't even know that elephants were killed by humans, and now they want it stopped. One student said, "We have to help them or they'll be extinct like dinosaurs!" For them to apply this new knowledge to something they have already learned (the words *extinct* and *endangered*) shows me that they are thinking at a deeper level about this content, and that is what I wanted for this kindergarten class.

5. What changes in students' knowledge and performance have occurred as a result of the service learning project?

The students are more aware of what *endangered* means. We also discussed products they could buy that don't have ivory in them. I've also seen them share facts about elephants with their other friends.

6. What changes in students' attitudes and behavior have occurred as a result of the service learning project?

While I was explaining that the mother elephants are killed for their tusks, leaving their babies all alone, the children became very concerned and emotional. After they finished the project, all of the students were proud of their work and they couldn't wait to hang it up around school.

7. What changes in students' enthusiasm/motivation have occurred as a result of the service learning project?

The students initially did not want to do a project. They thought it would be boring and uninteresting. After I described the trouble the elephants and their babies were in, the children's motivation completely changed. They were excited to be doing this activity and wanted others to know about it. One student asked, "What if people don't listen to us?" I told him some people won't listen, but we have to think about the people who *will* listen, not the few who won't. The students' posters were phenomenal! Some were so vivid; you could tell they really cared for the elephants. One student drew an elephant that had no tusks with tears coming out of its eyes.

8. Describe changes in the ways that students talk about service learning or the subject area of their project.

They talked about it constantly—on the playground, with their parents and older siblings. They wanted everyone to know what they were doing to help the elephants. The students have a lot of knowledge about this subject area now. One student from another class made a wrongful comment about the posters and my whole class bombarded him to let him know he was wrong. They also pointed out other facts that were in the picture.

9. Describe three specific student products and compare the quality of those products with other work by those students.

One student was very vivid in her work. She drew an elephant without tusks and tears coming down its face and wrote the words "Don't hurt the elephants!" Her work was amazing for her age; she is very artistically talented. Another student who does not talk much and is not usually able to complete an assignment drew a full picture of an elephant in a forest being hunted by poachers. Another student put a circle on the paper along with her name and that was all. However, it took her the entire time allotted just to do that, so compared to the other two students, artistic expression is not something she enjoys.

10. How did the service learning project support the standards?

This project supported the following science, social studies, and visual arts standards: Knows the activities of humans affect plants and animals in many ways; Knows the qualities of a good citizen; Uses two-dimensional and three-dimensional media, techniques, tools, and processes to depict works of art from personal experiences, observation, and imagination; Uses art materials and tools to develop basic processes and motor skills, in a safe and responsible manner; and Uses good craftsmanship when producing works of art.

11. Are you planning to use service learning in your future instruction?

I am definitely planning on using more service learning in my instruction. It went extremely well with the children and the final product turned out great.

12. What have been the major barriers to students participating in this service learning project?

Students at first were discouraged about having to draw an elephant, but I showed them a simple way to draw it and they picked it up quickly.

Sample Lesson Plan Matrix

Topic Area	Subjects Covered	Literacy	Math	Science	Social Studies	Creative Arts	Cognitive Development (PreK)	Social & Emotional Development (PreK)
Letter Writing	Grade							
Butterfly Cards for Seniors	PreK	X						
Letters to Soldiers	K–1	X		X				
Cards for Children in the Hospital	K–1	X		X	X			
Letters to Government Officials	2–3	X			X			
Letters and Support for Hurricane Victims	PreK–3	X		X	X			

Other ideas: Write a letter to a researcher about the environment, farming, education, etc.; write thank-you letters to school support personnel, community helpers, conservation groups, etc.

Topic Area								
Gardening Projects								
Growing Flowers for Others	PreK–1	X		X			X	
Beautifying Our School	PreK–3		X	X			X	
Butterfly Garden	K–1			X				
Flower Pens	PreK–3	X		X	X		X	

Other ideas: Study and plant native plants as a way of conserving natural resources; create miniature rainforests in jars

Topic Area								
Helping Others								
Second Harvest	PreK–3		X		X	X	X	
Helping Those in Need	K–1	X	X		X			
Habitats for Habitat for Humanity	PreK–3	X	X	X	X	X	X	X
Acts of Kindness	PreK–3	X					X	X

Other ideas: Hold a book drive or make teddy bears for children in the hospital; raise money and collect provisions for the Ronald McDonald House; collect school supplies, donations, and cards for victims of natural disasters

Topic Area								
Environmental Issues								
School Trash and Pollution	PreK–3	X	X		X	X		X
School Recycling	K–1	X		X				
Conservation Protects and Saves Animals	PreK–3	X		X			X	X

Other ideas: Study and observe the effects of pollution on marine animals; create posters to educate others about endangered animals; promote awareness of using wind energy in conservation efforts; raise money for the Children's Safe Drinking Water foundation (10-cent packets can clean bacteria from up to 10 liters of contaminated water)

PART FOUR

Supporting Research and Teacher Education

Chapter 13

Early Childhood Theorists and Service Learning

Chapter 2 provides a rationale for using service learning with young children. This chapter extends and builds upon that information by discussing the theories that provide solid support for the use of service learning in early childhood. It includes more in-depth analysis of the relation between the pedagogy of service learning and early childhood education theory, in particular *constructivism*. In the words of researcher Carol Kinsley, "Another way to understand how service learning can be used as a process of learning is to consider how it provides a way to implement the constructivist theory of education."[1] Constructivist education is the developmentally appropriate approach to early education, inspired by Jean Piaget's theory that the child constructs knowledge, intelligence, personality, and social and moral values. In this model, learning is an integrated process defined by exploration of the environment and the experience. In other words, experience is the best teacher: "While we only remember 10 percent of what we hear, 15 percent of what we see, and 20 percent of what we see and hear, we retain 60 percent of what we do, 80 percent of what is done actively with reflection, and 90 percent of what we teach others. Thus, the deep effects of service learning are likely due to its experiential and reflective nature."[2]

Our understanding of how children learn has been influenced and guided by a number of theories and theorists. The role of active experiences was emphasized by John Dewey early in the 20th century. Later, contributions by Jean Piaget, Lev Vygotsky, and others highlighted the importance of activity and experience in young children's learning. The work of these theorists contributed to the theory of constructivism, in which children play an active role in constructing new knowledge. While the constructivist view of learning lends support to the use of service learning with young learners, the contributions of researchers such as Lawrence Kohlberg, Carol Gilligan, Nel Noddings, and Thomas Lickona confirm the social, moral, and emotional benefits of service learning. The following sections highlight the contributions of each of these theorists, and how their work supports a service learning pedagogy for young children.

> Constructivist education is the developmentally appropriate approach to early education, inspired by Jean Piaget's theory that the child constructs knowledge, intelligence, personality, and social and moral values.

---

[1] Kinsley (1997), p. 4
[2] Wade & Anderson (1996), p. 62

John Dewey:
A Moral Education

John Dewey (1859–1952) was an American philosopher, psychologist, and educational reformer whose thoughts and ideas greatly influenced educational practice. Indeed, Dewey arguably made the most significant contribution to educational thinking in the 20th century. Guided by his belief that education should engage with and enlarge experience, Dewey emphasized the importance of informal and experiential education. He held the conviction that children should come to school to be in a community that provided them with guided experiences and real-life tasks and challenges that, in turn, foster their capacity to contribute to society. According to Dewey, learning from experience might be called "nature's way of learning." Drawing on Dewey's contribution, therefore, schools should provide opportunities for students to apply their learning to the community and the world at large. Opportunities for service learning give children a way to become involved in the community, while learning the fundamental skills and meeting the core objectives of the curriculum.

In his 1916 book *Democracy and Education,* Dewey outlines his theories of morals. He asserts that, "the moral and social quality of conduct are . . . identical with each other."[3] This is closely tied to service learning as both forms of conduct are based on interactions and experiences with others. Dewey also says that "what is learned and employed in an occupation having an aim and involving cooperation with others is moral knowledge, whether consciously so regarded or not."[4] He stated that moral behavior is determined by a set of values learned from lived experiences.

Furthermore, Dewey believed that moral education in schools rests upon the values that children bring to the educational setting, and that these values stem from the children's study of their own environments and communities. However, he did not believe that schools could directly teach specific morals. He claimed that by defining and teaching morals, schools define morality too narrowly. According to Dewey, moral behaviors are based directly on interactions with others and are as broad on each individual's lived experiences. Thus, schools should relate morality to actual conditions and problems facing the community.

Dewey asserts that schools can establish an effective moral education environment by creating a genuine community life. Teachers should combine the work and play of school through constructive activities because "they afford an opportunity for a social atmosphere." He also states that learning in school should be continuous with the learning out of school; if what is taught in school is not congruent with life outside of school, the moral lessons will not have a carryover effect. Schools and society should have a seamless fit, each reflecting the other. Education alone is not a means to a moral life.

> Drawing on Dewey's contribution, schools should provide opportunities for students to apply their learning to the community and the world at large.

Jean Piaget:
Submersion in Experience

In 1965, not long after the death of John Dewey, French developmental psychologist Jean Piaget (1896–1980) famously studied how thinking and learning develop in children via interview structures and marble playing. Based on his cognitive-developmental constructivist theory, Piaget believed that "learning is the active construction of knowledge through interactions with people and the environment that takes place in stages."[5] In other words, knowledge from text does not fully engage children in the learning experience. According to Piaget, most of the moral rules children learn to respect come from adults and are transmitted like language from generation to generation. However, each individual child makes the rules his or her own. Therefore, rather than merely reading

---

[3] Dewey (1916), p. 415
[4] ibid, p. 414
[5] Jalongo & Isenberg (2000), p. 133

about cooperation and interaction, service learning projects offer children the opportunities to expand their knowledge of the world around them by being actively involved, constructing knowledge, and creating their own understanding and rules.

Interacting in the community with a variety of people and resources offers children a vast pool of knowledge. As stated by the National Association for the Education of Young Children (NAEYC), one principle of child development and learning that describes developmentally appropriate practice is that "Children are active learners, drawing on direct physical and social experience as well as culturally transmitted knowledge to construct their own understandings of the world around them."[6] Piaget's constructivism justifies the effectiveness of service learning, as it includes theories regarding the importance of being directly involved in the learning experience.

Considering this perspective on how children learn, it is only practical to submerge students in a learning experience. Being submerged in the experience creates a relationship with the experience, and children learn and grow as citizens through the relationship. The NAEYC further states in DAP that "children develop and learn best in the context of a community where they are safe and valued, their physical needs are met, and they feel psychologically secure."[7] Service learning projects offer children avenues to the community, while remaining safe and cared for by school rules and among people they can trust.

Lev Vygotsky: Socially Constructed Learning

Another theorist whose work greatly supports the usefulness of service learning is Russian psychologist Lev Semenovich Vygotsky (1896–1934). Vygotsky, a peer of Piaget's, developed what is called the sociocultural constructivist theory. He believed that all learning is socially constructed. Learning first occurs socially between children, and then occurs inside the child. A child's mind is directly shaped by the knowledge systems, tools, and practices found within the practices of his or her social world or culture. The sociocultural

theory emphasizes the importance of social interaction. It stresses "social activity and cultural practice as the basis of thinking, the centrality of pedagogy in development, and the inseparability of the person from the social context."[8] In short, why search far for knowledge, when it can be learned by interacting with one's immediate surroundings?

In order to create a community of learners, Vygotsky suggests that early childhood settings should include discovery and guided learning experiences with ample opportunities for dialogue between children and adults. Most service learning projects include hands-on discovery, sharing of ideas, interactive teaching, and cooperative learning.

> The ultimate goal, to be "good and smart," can be reached as students learn core curricular standards through community involvement and relationship building.

Lawrence Kohlberg: Moral Reasoning

The contributions of Jewish-American psychologist Lawrence Kohlberg (1927–1987) have also influenced service learning in early childhood education. Kohlberg, who extended the work of Piaget, became a leader in moral education as he analyzed the maturing of moral reasoning. He believed that a person's ethical behavior progressed through stages of moral reasoning. These stages are divided into three levels: pre-conventional, conventional, and post-conventional, and span from simple obedience and obligation to social mutuality and principled conscience.

Kohlberg attempted to capture and label the logic behind specific actions and virtues and thereby define one's level of moral reasoning. Such virtues as honesty, integrity, fairness, respect, and responsibility can be taught and practiced through service learning projects. Furthermore, children will gain moral reasoning and excel through Kohlberg's stages as the focus shifts from self to others. The ultimate goal, to be "good and smart," can be reached as students learn core curricular

---

[6] Bredekamp & Copple (1997), p. 13
[7] ibid., p. 15
[8] Bodrova & Leong (1996), p. 136

standards through community involvement and relationship building. Each student prioritizes particular virtues, which can develop a more encompassing character that pertains to his or her interests, beliefs, and experiences.

Character education, and particularly moral reasoning, occurs as a "hidden curriculum" when students unintentionally practice personal virtues through service learning projects. Kohlberg states that "education for development is not achieved through direct teaching and instruction . . . the child employs thinking that is self-generated and that changes gradually."[9] For example, actively involving the school community in recycling is a much more effective lesson than simply learning facts about recycling. Being involved allows children to reflect and gain personal experience and understanding of morals. Furthermore, helping others inadvertently helps the children work through Kohlberg's stages of moral development. As is commonly stated, true service learning is designed to help the servers as much as those who are being served.

Carol Gilligan and Grant Wiggins: Justice and Care

In the 1980s, researchers Carol Gilligan and Grant Wiggins also studied the moral development of young children. They identified two dimensions of early childhood relationships that shape young children's awareness of self in relation to others. "One is the dimension of inequality, reflected in the child's awareness of being smaller and less capable than adults and older children, of being a baby in relation to a standard of human being."[10] This dimension is characterized by a feeling of helplessness and powerlessness relative to others, due to young children being dependent on those who are bigger and more powerful. Therefore, some psychologists identify morality with justice, and align development with the child's progress toward equality and independence. The second dimension focuses on the child's attachments and the dynamics of the attachment relationship. Attachment

relationships "create a different awareness of self—as capable of having an effect on others, as able to move others and be moved by them."[11] These two dimensions of inequality and attachments form the basis of two moral visions—one of justice and one of care.

The lessons learned about justice and care in early childhood relationships generate expectations that are confirmed or modified in later childhood and adolescence. Two moral injunctions—to treat others fairly and to help others in need—define two lines of moral development, providing different standards for assessing moral judgments and moral behavior and pointing to changes in the understanding of what fairness means and what constitutes care. Clearly, service learning offers the perfect context and foundation for young children to build on their moral values by learning to treat others fairly and helping those in need.

Nel Noddings: The Ethic of Care

In contrast to Lawrence Kohlberg's stages of moral reasoning, feminist theorist Nel Noddings argues that women use more than just logic when making moral decisions; they take into account affective elements such as feelings, hopes, and desires. In other words, they *care*. When presented with hypothetical moral dilemmas like those found in Kohlberg's research, women often ask for more information, attempting to most closely resemble real-life situations. Women "need to talk to the participants, to see their eyes and facial expressions, and to receive what they are feeling,"[12] wrote Noddings in her 1984 book *Caring: A Feminist Approach to Ethics and Moral Education*.

Children and preservice teachers, like all of us, need practice in caring. Noddings suggests that one way for students to gain this practice is to engage in regular service activities in the school or community. "Wherever students might be assigned—to hospitals, nursing homes, animal shelters, parks, botanical gardens—a definite expectation would be that their work be a true apprenticeship in caring."[13] Students should be offered opportunities to learn to care for humans and animals directly and indirectly, through helping and maintaining the

[9] Kohlberg & Selman (1972), p. 24
[10] Gilligan & Wiggins (1988), p. 114
[11] ibid.
[12] Noddings (1984), p. 2–3
[13] ibid, p. 187

4

environment. Noddings further explains that this service can be a practical way for some students to practice skills that they may be struggling with in the academic setting. In addition to involving students in service to their school and community, Noddings also encourages teachers to allow children to cooperate with each other as a way to practice caring. Classroom strategies such as group work, cooperative structures, and cooperative learning are among a few that might be useful. In addition to fostering caring encounters, these strategies enable students to learn from their peers and foster a sense of classroom unity.

> Lickona emphasizes the importance of service when he explains that to develop the values of responsibility and caring, children (and preservice teachers) must first *have* responsibility and *perform* caring deeds.

Thomas Lickona: Promoting Awareness

In *Educating for Character: How Our Schools Can Teach Respect and Responsibility* (1992), developmental psychologist Thomas Lickona discusses the controversial issue of values education in our public schools. He offers practical strategies for teachers to improve their students' moral character. He also stresses that effective values education needs to go beyond the classroom and become a school effort. Lickona offers many strategies for children to learn respect and responsibility outside of the classroom, and it is this area of his work that directly relates to service learning.

According to Lickona, children need to become aware of the problems facing their community, country, or world, before they can be expected to help. Teachers need to help facilitate this awareness in their early childhood and preservice classrooms. Lickona emphasizes the importance of service when he explains that to develop

the values of responsibility and caring, children (and preservice teachers) must first *have* responsibility and *perform* caring deeds. "Simply learning about the value of caring may increase students' moral knowledge. But it won't necessarily develop their own commitment to that value, their confidence that they themselves can help, or the skills needed to help effectively."[14]

When considering the optimal expectations of future generations, ultimately, society does not demand much. Thomas Lickona is often quoted in saying, "Down through history and all over the world, education has had two great goals: to help people become smart and to help them become good."[15] Martin Luther King Jr. once said, "Intelligence is not enough. Intelligence plus character, that is the goal of true education." Academic learning may allow us to become smart, but human character is what allows us to experiment with being good. Integrating service learning into the early childhood school curriculum and preservice teacher curriculum builds this character and can guide our future generations to fulfill academic objectives while supporting and being involved in the community.

Chapter Summary

The works of several theorists lend support to the use of service learning in early childhood education. Dewey was a proponent of experiential learning who believed that children should be given an opportunity to apply their learning in their communities and use their skills for the greater good. Piaget's cognitive developmental theories also support the role of experience in children's learning. For Vygotsky, learning is a social process and interaction with others is important in guiding and shaping children's thinking and learning. The importance of a service learning approach for developing attitudes, values, and morals is supported by the works of Kohlberg, Gilligan and Wiggins, Noddings, and Lickona. The theories discussed in this chapter continue to be highly regarded by early childhood teachers because of their emphasis on first-hand learning and child-initiated, age-appropriate experiences. Most important is the fact that these theories support the notion that learning is an active process that is influenced by the learner, the teacher, and the community.

---

[14] Lickona (1991), p. 312
[15] ibid., p. 67

Chapter 14

Service Learning in Professional Development and Teacher Education

Now that you have read about the benefits of service learning and how to design service learning for young children, we hope you are inspired to initiate service learning projects on your own. Just like any other educational endeavor, the success or failure of service learning projects ultimately depends on *you*, the teacher. You design the service learning project, you guide students in implementing the project, and you interact with students as they reflect on their projects. That is why integrating service learning into all stages of teacher education and development is vitally important.

The following chapter can be used in a number of different settings in which teachers at all levels can be educated about service learning. If you're a classroom teacher of grades preK to three, you may participate in some kind of professional development program in your school or district, sometimes called a PLC, or professional learning community. A PLC is a great place to discuss, introduce others to, and advance your own practice of service learning by using the information and forms provided here. Likewise, if you are a preservice teacher or a faculty member in a college or university early education program, this chapter can help you seamlessly integrate service learning into your college courses.

During the past several years we have worked with both preservice and in-service early childhood classroom teachers to provide them with the knowledge, skills, and dispositions to successfully use service learning with young children. Through working with these professionals, we have identified effective ways to support teachers as they learn about service learning in early childhood, which we discuss in this chapter.

> Integrating service learning into all stages of teacher education and development is vitally important.

Service Learning and Empowerment

A key concept throughout this chapter is that of *empowerment*. A sense of empowerment can emerge from any level of participation in service learning. The following vignette highlights how a successful service learning project led to a feeling of empowerment in one preservice teacher and her kindergarten students.

"For my service learning project, we raised money to send to AIDS victims in Darfur, Africa. The kindergarten students watched a video portraying different aspects of Darfur, and located Africa and Darfur on a world map. We created a graph to track the amount of money brought in by the students, and each morning we counted the money and added it to the graph. The students were encouraged to 'earn' the money they brought in by doing chores, etc. When the students brought money in, they told the class what they did to 'earn' their money. This service learning project focused on helping people suffering from disease who do not have food to eat, clothes to wear, or a school to attend. The students gained an understanding that not all people are as fortunate as many are here in the United States. They wanted to help make a difference. Their attitude toward the project was amazing! Before we began the project, they knew little about how others are not as privileged, and so they were not as eager to help them. My students got a lot out of this project. They were so excited every time we talked about it. This project was the best part of my field experience. I know now that I'm going to use service learning when I have my own class."

—Preservice teacher, grade K

Empowerment is a term that captures one of the most important outcomes of service learning in early childhood. Quality service learning projects can lead to empowerment of all participants: teachers, students, parents, administrators, and community partners. "Empowerment is a process that challenges our assumptions about the way things are and can be. It challenges our basic assumptions about power, helping, achieving, and succeeding."[1]

As a teacher or teacher educator, you must feel empowered by service learning before you can help young children or preservice teachers feel empowered in your classroom. In her book *Roots and Wings: Affirming Culture in Early Childhood Programs,* author Stacey York outlines the steps teachers go through in order to feel confident and gain awareness of multicultural education. The steps taken by teachers and teacher educators to feel empowered through service learning follow the same path:

Six Steps to Teacher Empowerment Through Service Learning

1. Bring your knowledge of child development, early childhood practices, and experiences to the service learning project.

2. Increase your awareness of personal experiences, attitudes, biases, and societal oppression. (Stage 1: Investigation)

3. Establish or renew your belief in or commitment to service learning, and then set project goals. (Stage 2: Preparation)

4. Carry out the service learning project to effect change in the environment. (Stage 3: Action)

5. Reflect on the service learning project (e.g., how well did you incorporate the project into the existing curriculum?), solve problems, and revise methods. (Stage 4: Reflection)

6. Demonstrate that you have achieved the goals of the service learning project by sharing the skills, insights, and outcomes with another group. (Stage 5: Demonstration)

---

[1] Page & Czuba (1999), p. 1

Following these steps of empowerment allows you to successfully implement service learning into your early childhood or university classroom. Empowering yourself as a teacher or teacher educator involves formulating your own knowledge and opinions and taking an active role in your classroom. Feeling empowered stems from taking a stand and trying to make a difference. Through service learning, both you and your students are given opportunities to take a stand and help others, expand your virtues through individual experiences, and gain control and ownership over your actions. In short, service learning helps educators develop a system that will undoubtedly lead to a classroom community of, in the words of Thomas Lickona, *good* and *smart* children.

Service Learning and Early Childhood Teacher Education

In recent years, many early childhood classrooms have moved toward skills-based instruction and away from practices that integrate curriculum. In these classrooms, service learning can be a way of introducing, maintaining, or keeping appropriate practices for young children. For teacher educators, service learning can act as a "backdoor entry" for preservice teachers to apply constructivist, experiential, or integrated practices with children. Classrooms should be learner-centered and knowledge-centered environments that focus equally on the child, subject matter, understanding, curriculum, and learning goals.

Rationales for Service Learning

In the book *Service Learning in Teacher Education,* Susan Verducci and Denise Clark Pope compiled in their article the five most cited rationales for including service learning in teacher education programs. Following, we discuss these reasons and describe how we, as university professors, have met (or attempted to meet) them in practice.

1. **Service learning in teacher education enhances preservice teachers' teaching and learning by improving their understanding of the academic content.** The service learning projects we've implemented enable preservice teachers to use a variety of effective teaching

strategies with their children, plan for learning outside of the regular classrooms, and make connections between their content courses and the specific curriculum in their field classrooms.

2. **Service learning in teacher education increases preservice teachers' civic understanding, participation, and transformation.** Several of the service learning projects in our program were chosen because the preservice teachers were passionate about or had a personal connection to the project topic. Through researching and teaching the projects, the preservice teachers shared their knowledge, stories, and passion with others, thus continuing their civic transformation.

3. **Service learning in teacher education promotes social, moral, and personal benefits for preservice teachers.** Service learning has been found to positively promote issues of tolerance, self-esteem, and sensitivity. It is especially important for the preservice teachers in our program—who mostly come from white, middle- and upper-middle-class backgrounds—to be versed in methods that are effective for diverse learners and that teach tolerance.

4. **Service learning in teacher education prepares preservice teachers for the workforce by having them work with children with whom they might otherwise not work with.** In our preservice teachers' first semester, their community partner is the local homeless coalition. Together, they plan service learning projects that meet the needs of the community and also match the early childhood goals of our program.

5. **Service learning in teacher education assists preservice teachers in meeting the national and state standards.** The service learning projects created by the preservice teachers in our program integrated and taught many of the state and national content standards. Moreover, integrating service learning into our teacher education program enabled us to meet several of the National Council for Accreditation of Teacher Education (NCATE) standards.

In addition to producing the five outcomes just listed, when service learning is used in structured ways with preservice teachers, it helps them do the following:

- apply academic, social, and personal skills to improve or supplement instruction

- make decisions that have real, not hypothetical, results

- grow as individuals and cooperative groups, gain respect for peers, and increase civic participation

- experience success no matter what their ability level

- gain a deeper understanding of themselves, their community, and society

- develop as leaders who take initiative, solve problems, and work as a team[2]

Incorporating Service Learning into Teacher Education and Professional Development: Where to Begin?

Clearly, there are compelling reasons for integrating early childhood teacher education and service learning. But as a teacher or teacher educator, you may wonder where to begin. In her book *The Complete Guide to Service Learning*, Cathryn Berger Kaye offers these suggestions for classroom teachers beginning to use service learning with their students:

1. Identify an existing program or activity and go from there.

2. Begin with the standard curriculum and find a natural extension.

3. Plan a theme or unit of study and identify content or skill connections.

4. Start with a student-identified need or a school- or community-identified need.[3]

These same suggestions can be used at the university level when introducing preservice teachers to service learning, or when educating members of a school or district professional learning community (PLC) about service learning. In addition, the following two methods are helpful.

Use a Cascading Model of Integration

The cascading model uses the service learning method itself to teach pre- and in-service teachers about service learning pedagogy. A cascading model also involves the application of service learning with young children, so that teachers learn about the approach through firsthand experiences. Such an approach allows service learning to be efficiently integrated across all program areas, including course work, class assignments, field experiences, and internships.

A cascading service learning model starts at the university level with the teacher educators instructing the preservice teachers about service learning and also participating in service learning. Then the next level is to have preservice teachers design service learning projects and implement them with young children. The preservice teachers offer young children hands-on and appropriate service learning opportunities so that they can learn in ways that are most natural to them, as opposed to a segmented approach stressing isolated skills and concepts.

Likewise, in a professional learning community, you might use the cascading model of integration by involving PLC members in a service learning project with a class or group of children.

Develop Teachers' Personal Connections

Another approach to integration is to weave the ideas of service learning into the students' existing ideas in an early childhood education classroom. Preservice teachers have mental models about children's minds, how learning takes place, and their roles as teachers. Therefore, an integrated approach of service learning and courses in early childhood methods would allow instructors to focus in greater detail on developing preservice teachers' own personal connections between service learning and the regular curriculum. Preservice teachers would then use these connections to better understand and influence children's constructions of curricular concepts and skills. An integrated approach to early childhood methods courses would more likely reflect the realities of teaching, thereby allowing preservice teachers to shape their emerging understanding of teaching.

---

[2] Bringle, Phillips, & Husdon (2004); Howard (2003); Kaye (2010)
[3] Kaye (2010), p. 25–26

This same method is also appropriate when introducing or reinforcing service learning in a PLC, thus shaping members' existing mental models and beliefs. Simply insert service learning connections into discussions already being held in member meetings.

Principles of Good Practice

In their book chapter "Principles of Good Practice for Service-Learning in Preservice Teacher Education," Jeffrey Anderson and Don Hill outline 10 principles of good practice for integrating service learning with teacher education curriculum. Service learning leaders and teacher educators from across the United States developed these principles. They assert that these principles are not to be applied rigidly, but are to be used as a knowledge base when considering service learning in your courses. The authors have found few teacher education programs that incorporate all 10 principles, but state that "the successful integration of any one of these principles will strengthen service learning activities, and they are therefore beneficial for those new to service learning as well as for experienced practitioners."[4]

You can also review or study these principles with your PLC, regardless of members' levels of expertise with service learning.

Principle 1

Preservice teachers should prepare to use service learning as pedagogy by participating in service learning experiences as well as studying the content of service learning. Unless beginning teachers receive explicit instruction on *what* service learning is and *how* to implement service learning in field settings, they will be less likely to use service learning in their own classrooms.

Principle 2

Teacher education faculty involved in service learning need to have a clear understanding of service learning theory and principles of good practice, and actually be modeling these for their students. Teacher educators also need to be involved in service learning research in order to stay current in the latest findings and to contribute to the knowledge base. Teacher educators must be role models or service learning will not be effective.

Principle 3

Teacher education courses that include service learning should be utilizing theories and practices that are congruent to service learning. Courses taken by preservice teachers should model construction of knowledge, experiential learning, and active learning that is connected to the course objectives. Lecturing to students or disseminating information while they are passive learners is not a match to service learning.

Principle 4

The design, implementation, and evaluation of service learning should reflect everyone involved: preservice teachers, students, and community members. This type of communication requires extensive collaboration and trust between all partners involved and is often accomplished after several semesters or years of working together.

Principle 5

Reciprocity and respect should be present between the teacher education program, schools, and community. All parties must have clear goals and responsibilities for the service learning, especially pertaining to the supervision and evaluation of preservice teachers.

Principle 6

Preservice teachers should participate in many service learning experiences that include diverse populations. Service learning experiences should be included in several courses so the preservice teachers have the opportunity to expand and increase their knowledge and vary their experiences.

Principle 7

Preservice teachers should engage in a plethora of frequent and structured reflection activities and be taught how to implement reflection activities with their future students. Doing is not enough; one must process and synthesize the information and ideas gained through the service learning experience by reflecting on the experience. Reflection should be tied to course objectives and the curriculum.

Principle 8

Preservice teachers should learn how to use formative and summative assessments in order to enhance and measure service learning student outcomes. Teacher educators should use and model assessment tools so preservice teachers will understand that assessment is a natural part of service learning.

Principle 9

Teacher educators should align service learning objectives with program goals and state and national standards for teacher certification and program accreditation. Linking service learning to program accreditation and certification standards helps to ensure that, while program faculty shift and change, program integrity will remain intact.

Principle 10

The teacher education program, institution, and community should support service learning by providing resources necessary for its success. Avenues of support include:

- an institutionalized service learning mission
- faculty rewards and reduced workload
- long-term commitment to service learning from the institution
- public support of service learning from all levels of administration
- a service learning coordinator appointed in schools and universities
- a service learning budget
- time to engage in service learning
- safety considerations for preservice teachers and faculty to engage in service learning[5]

Preservice Teacher Forms and Templates

The following forms and templates are ones we have found useful as teacher educators. We thought it might be helpful for you to see the forms first before we share our story of implementing service learning at the program level and in one of our courses (see pages 193–199).

- **Before I Begin: Preservice Teacher Survey** (page 176). This is a great tool to use if you are a preservice teacher just starting to learn about service learning. Take it at the beginning of the semester so you will have baseline data on your knowledge of service learning. If you are not a preservice teacher, modify the language of this survey to suit your needs.

Preservice Teacher Service Learning Assessments

Unlike assessments for children, there is no shortage of assessments for college or university students. For those readers who are involved with early childhood service learning at the college level, we have included four different documents ranging from surveys to a more reflective set of questions. Pick and choose what works for you; use them as they are, modify them, or combine them. The important thing is to find a tool that is a match to your needs and your program.

- **Preservice Teacher Evaluation of Service Learning Course Component** (pages 177–178) is a survey assessment using a four-level Likert scale. Questions are general and cover such topics as the ability to apply class concepts to a service learning experience, service learning group contributions and experiences, service learning satisfaction, and college course satisfaction.

- **Preservice Teacher Assessment of Growth Obtained by Participating in a Service Learning Project** (pages 179–182). The first eight questions ask the students to rate their personal experiences using a four-level Likert scale. Next are community questions with a comment section, followed by information regarding how service learning was used in their course.

- **Preservice Teacher Evaluation of Service Learning and Its Importance** (pages 183–186) is a survey that asks the student to agree or disagree with each of the items and then rate each of the items on its importance to him or her. The questions range from value assessments, to communication skills, to political and social assumptions, to the appreciation of cultural norms.

---

[5] ibid.

- **Preservice Teacher Assessment of Service Learning Experience and Site** (pages 187–189) is a short-answer evaluation concentrating on the impact of service learning groups on a particular site. It also asks for critical feedback about working at the site and if service learning should continue to be used at the site and in the course.

- **Teacher Assessment of the Service Learning Project** (pages 113–114). We have found this evaluation to be very effective for preservice teachers as well as in-service teachers, especially when combined with the **Child-to-Child Evaluation of Service Learning** (pages 104–105). The preservice teachers should answer the questions in several sentences (sometimes more), evaluating the effectiveness of their service learning experience.

College Faculty Assessments and Evaluations

These college faculty member evaluations offer two different choices: survey or reflective questions. Depending on your faculty members, you will know which one to use. Add, modify, or delete questions to make these forms your own.

- **College Faculty Member Service Learning Satisfaction Survey** (page 190) is a 12-question survey using a four-level Likert scale. Questions range from teaching strategies, to instructional time, to personal satisfaction.

- **College Faculty Member Service Learning Assessment** (pages 191–192) asks the faculty members to evaluate the service learning by answering 10 questions about the service learning experience and how they incorporated it into their courses.

Before I Begin: Preservice Teacher Survey

Directions: Respond to the following questions using the scale below.

4 = Strongly Agree   **3 = Agree**   **2 = Disagree**   **1 = Strongly Disagree**

1. I can identify many of the challenges facing the community in which I live.	4	3	2	1
2. I believe that caring and committed people can work together to improve the community.	4	3	2	1
3. I have a responsibility to serve my community.	4	3	2	1
4. I learn best when I am able to connect course content to real-world concepts.	4	3	2	1
5. I understand the difference between service learning and volunteering.	4	3	2	1
6. It excites me to know that I can make a difference in my community while increasing my knowledge of the course content.	4	3	2	1

7. This will be my first service learning experience. (Please circle) Yes / No

8. Below is an explanation of my first service learning project.

9. I chose this activity because . . .

Preservice Teacher Evaluation of Service Learning Course Component

Name: Date:

Course:

Service Learning Site/School:

Directions: The questions below relate specifically to the service learning component within this course. Your responses will help the instructor improve and modify the service learning experience in future semesters. Beside each statement, rate your level of satisfaction with the service learning experiences you participated in this semester.

4 = Strongly Agree   **3 = Agree**   **2 = Disagree**   **1 = Strongly Disagree**

1. I was able to apply the concepts I learned in class to the service learning experience.	4	3	2	1
2. The service learning experience helped me better understand some of the concepts presented in the course.	4	3	2	1
3. Enough time was spent in class preparing me for my service learning experience.	4	3	2	1
4. The time spent on the service learning project was reasonable.	4	3	2	1
5. Each member of my group contributed to the service learning experience.	4	3	2	1
6. My group worked well together.	4	3	2	1
7. Service learning in this course strengthened the learning experience.	4	3	2	1
8. Service learning is an important concept in college-level education curriculum.	4	3	2	1

continued

9. I will look for education courses in the future that have a service learning component.	4	3	2	1
10. Overall, I am satisfied with the service learning experience in this course.	4	3	2	1

About how many children or adults did you work with in your service learning project?

Approximately how many hours did you spend on your project or at your service learning site?

Briefly describe your service learning project:

Preservice Teacher Assessment of Growth Obtained by Participating in a Service Learning Project

Directions: Rate your personal experience using the scale below.

4 = **Strongly Agree**   3 = **Agree**   2 = **Disagree**   1 = **Strongly Disagree**

1. I have interacted with people from different cultures that I would not have interacted with had I not had this experience.	4	3	2	1
2. I have an appreciation for different cultures that I did not have before this experience.	4	3	2	1
3. I have developed relationships with people from different cultures I did not have before this experience.	4	3	2	1
4. I have experienced different social and economic environments because of this experience.	4	3	2	1
5. This experience has influenced my attitude toward communities that are different from my own.	4	3	2	1
6. My service experience has increased my interpersonal skills.	4	3	2	1
7. My service experience has given me an appreciation for what I have.	4	3	2	1
8. My service experience has caused me to view people and communities in a different context.	4	3	2	1

continued

Preservice Teacher Assessment of Growth Obtained by Participating in a Service Learning Project (continued)

Directions: Rate your level of satisfaction with the following using this scale:

4 = Very Satisfied   3 = Satisfied   2 = Dissatisfied   1 = Very Dissatisfied   N/A = Not Applicable

	4	3	2	1	N/A
9. Your service learning experience: Comment:	4	3	2	1	N/A
10. Your service learning team: Comment:	4	3	2	1	N/A
11. Your community service site: Comment:	4	3	2	1	N/A

continued

Preservice Teacher Assessment of Growth Obtained by Participating in a Service Learning Project (continued)

12. Please rate how each issue has hindered your ability to perform service learning using this scale:

4 = Has hindered me greatly   1 = Has not hindered me at all   N/A = Not Applicable

Transportation	4	3	2	1	N/A
Service learning personnel	4	3	2	1	N/A
Variability in service times	4	3	2	1	N/A
Available free time	4	3	2	1	N/A
Work/school schedule	4	3	2	1	N/A
Variety/number of agencies	4	3	2	1	N/A
Cooperating teacher	4	3	2	1	N/A
School placement	4	3	2	1	N/A
Service learning work group	4	3	2	1	N/A
Administration support	4	3	2	1	N/A
Other (please specify)	4	3	2	1	N/A

13. What is your biggest complaint regarding your service learning experience?

continued ➡

14. How many site visits did your service learning experience involve?

_____ one time at the site

_____ 2–3 times at the site

_____ more than 3 times at the site

15. What obligation did your service fulfill?

_____ Class

_____ Scholarship

_____ Student organization (please specify) _____

_____ Other (please specify) _____

16. Will you continue your service at the same site next quarter, semester, or year?

_____ Yes

_____ No

Please Explain:

17. In your opinion, how have you changed as a direct result of your community service?
(e.g., "I'm more patient with children." "I'm less judgmental." "I haven't really changed much.")

Preservice Teacher Evaluation of Service Learning and Its Importance

Name: _____   Year: _____

Major: _____

Service Learning Experience: _____

Directions: For both columns, please check the box that corresponds with the response that *best* describes your experience.

4 = Strongly Agree/Very Important   1 = Strongly Disagree/Not Important   N/A = Not Applicable

This experience helped me:	Agree/Disagree:					How Important to Me:				
1. Gain skills and experience that will be valuable in my career.	4	3	2	1	N/A	4	3	2	1	N/A
2. Complement what I learned in the classroom.	4	3	2	1	N/A	4	3	2	1	N/A
3. Learn about myself.	4	3	2	1	N/A	4	3	2	1	N/A
4. Volunteer my time to help people.	4	3	2	1	N/A	4	3	2	1	N/A
5. Make a difference with issues of local, national, or global importance.	4	3	2	1	N/A	4	3	2	1	N/A
6. Develop a better understanding of the concepts important to be effective in this experience.	4	3	2	1	N/A	4	3	2	1	N/A

continued

Preservice Teacher Evaluation of Service Learning and Its Importance (continued)

This experience helped me:	Agree/Disagree:					How Important to Me:				
7. Understand the connection between the themes I have studied in class and this experience.	4	3	2	1	N/A	4	3	2	1	N/A
8. Learn to apply principles from my courses to new situations.	4	3	2	1	N/A	4	3	2	1	N/A
9. Gain a better understanding of my values and personal attitudes.	4	3	2	1	N/A	4	3	2	1	N/A
10. Gain a better understanding of my strengths and weaknesses.	4	3	2	1	N/A	4	3	2	1	N/A
11. Gained more self-confidence.	4	3	2	1	N/A	4	3	2	1	N/A
12. Assess my own assumptions about social, political, and economic issues.	4	3	2	1	N/A	4	3	2	1	N/A
13. Become more tolerant of people who have different backgrounds and lifestyles than me.	4	3	2	1	N/A	4	3	2	1	N/A
14. Cope more effectively with stress and real-life difficulties.	4	3	2	1	N/A	4	3	2	1	N/A
15. Learn, understand, and respect professional and business standards.	4	3	2	1	N/A	4	3	2	1	N/A

continued

Preservice Teacher Evaluation of Service Learning
and Its Importance (continued)

This experience helped me:	Agree/Disagree:					How Important to Me:				
16. Understand and appreciate different cultural norms.	4	3	2	1	N/A	4	3	2	1	N/A
17. Improve my written communication skills.	4	3	2	1	N/A	4	3	2	1	N/A
18. Improve my verbal communication skills.	4	3	2	1	N/A	4	3	2	1	N/A
19. Enhance my ability to lead a group.	4	3	2	1	N/A	4	3	2	1	N/A
20. Develop my capacity for independent learning.	4	3	2	1	N/A	4	3	2	1	N/A
21. Enhance my ability to understand different points of view.	4	3	2	1	N/A	4	3	2	1	N/A
22. Work more effectively as a team member.	4	3	2	1	N/A	4	3	2	1	N/A
23. Refine my ability to articulate new ideas.	4	3	2	1	N/A	4	3	2	1	N/A
24. Increase my capacity to make moral and ethical judgments.	4	3	2	1	N/A	4	3	2	1	N/A
25. Express dissenting opinions.	4	3	2	1	N/A	4	3	2	1	N/A
26. Learn appropriate ways to deal with conflict.	4	3	2	1	N/A	4	3	2	1	N/A

continued

Preservice Teacher Evaluation of Service Learning and Its Importance (continued)

This experience helped me:	Agree/Disagree:					How Important to Me:				
27. Become inspired to remain more informed about local, national, and international issues.	4	3	2	1	N/A	4	3	2	1	N/A
28. Want to engage others in identifying and proposing solutions concerning social, economic, or political issues.	4	3	2	1	N/A	4	3	2	1	N/A
29. Plan to use service learning as a way of teaching in my future classrooms.	4	3	2	1	N/A	4	3	2	1	N/A
30. Plan to stay involved with service projects and activities in the future and work to involve my family and friends.	4	3	2	1	N/A	4	3	2	1	N/A

Comments:

Preservice Teacher Assessment of Service Learning Experience and Site

1. Cite one example of how your group made an impact at your service learning site.

2. Briefly explain how your group related and worked together.

3. Check the response(s) below that best reflects what you learned as a result of your service learning experiences in this course.

_____ I learned how to put theory into practice.

_____ I gained a new perspective on how connections are made between the classroom and the real world.

_____ I learned that hands-on learning is important to learning new concepts.

_____ I now find it easier to understand class material.

_____ I learned that service learning enhances and expands the importance of class lectures.

_____ I learned the benefits of collaborative teamwork.

_____ I gained valuable opportunities to practice what I learned in class.

_____ Other (please explain) _____

continued ➡

Preservice Teacher Assessment of Service Learning Experience and Site (continued)

4. Check the response(s) below that best reflects what problem(s) you experienced with this course and/or with service learning.

_____ I had no problems.

_____ Not all team members played an equal part.

_____ Scheduling conflicts occurred with my team members.

_____ Scheduling conflicts occurred with the site.

_____ We started too late in the semester.

_____ Other (please explain) _____

5. Do you think service learning in this course should be changed or remain the same?

_____ Keep service learning as it is in this course.

_____ Change service learning in this course.

6. Please briefly explain what you particularly liked about service learning and what you would recommend be changed to enhance the experience.

7. Would you take another course that included service learning? Why or why not?

continued

8. What community sites were used that **should not be used** as future service learning sites? Why? List contact names and information.

9. What are project ideas that were not implemented this semester that should be considered for future semesters?

10. Other ideas:

College Faculty Member Service Learning Satisfaction Survey

Directions: Please circle the number that most accurately describes your opinion regarding the statements below.

4 = Strongly Agree　　　**3 = Agree**　　　**2 = Disagree**　　　**1 = Strongly Disagree**

1. Service learning proved to be a teaching strategy that enhanced my ability to communicate the objectives of the subject matter I teach.	4	3	2	1
2. The service my students completed through this class was beneficial to the community.	4	3	2	1
3. Using service learning was worth the time required of me as a teacher.	4	3	2	1
4. The service the students completed interfered with their academic responsibilities.	4	3	2	1
5. The idea of combining service to the community with college course work should be practiced in more classes at my college.	4	3	2	1
6. I received assistance with the mechanics of service learning (identifying placement sites, follow-up with students, etc.).	4	3	2	1
7. This experience made me more interested in doing service in my community than I was before.	4	3	2	1
8. Service learning fits in with all of the courses that I teach.	4	3	2	1
9. I will probably use service learning as a teaching strategy in future courses.	4	3	2	1
10. I learned more about my students through service learning than through classroom participation.	4	3	2	1
11. I learned much about myself through my service learning activities.	4	3	2	1
12. Some educators say that real learning means being able to integrate learning into your own behavior. Using that definition, this class was very successful in helping my students really learn.	4	3	2	1

Adapted from the American Association of Community Colleges as part of the CHESP grant, Florida.

From *Service Learning in the PreK–3 Classroom: The What, Why, and How-To Guide for Every Teacher* by Vickie E. Lake, Ph.D., and Ithel Jones, Ed.D., copyright © 2012. Free Spirit Publishing Inc., Minneapolis, MN; 800-735-7323; www.freespirit.com. This page may be reproduced for use within an individual school or district. For all other uses, contact www.freespirit.com/company/permissions.cfm.

College Faculty Member Service Learning Assessment

1. What have you learned from adding a service learning component to your course?

2. How are your students benefiting? (personally, academically, occupationally)

3. How does the quality of learning with service learning compare to traditional classroom learning?

4. What has the service learning option replaced, if anything, in your courses?

5. What would you change to improve your service learning option?

6. What criteria do you use to fulfill the service learning option?

continued

7. How many service learning hours do you require in your course?

8. Explain your service learning reflection and documentation components:

Written work:

Oral presentation:

Other reflection methods:

9. What percentage of the course grade is the service learning option?

10. Is there an option for extra points?

An Example of Service Learning in Early Childhood Teacher Education

In this section we describe how we implemented a cascading model of service learning across an early childhood teacher education program and how our children's literature course used children's books as springboards to classroom service learning projects. As you read about this program, notice the many different layers of service:

- The preservice teachers engage in service learning by working with young children in kindergarten and first-grade classrooms.

- The mentors (in-service classroom teachers) provide service to the undergraduate students by sharing their expertise with them.

- Senior preservice teachers engage in service not only in the classroom with young children, but also by helping and supporting their junior peers as they take their first tentative steps as teachers.

- Finally, the preservice teachers, with support from their mentors, design and implement service learning projects with the children. Here, the new teachers hone their skills as providers and recipients of service.

The structure of our early childhood program allows for a large amount of time for preservice teachers to be engaged in transforming theory into practice. They spend this time in early childhood classrooms each semester. In March of their sophomore year, undergraduate students apply to the early childhood program. Thirty applicants are selected and admitted to the program for the following fall semester. Once admitted, the students' classes are blocked and they travel together as a cohort of preservice teachers for the next four semesters, or blocks, until graduation.

A Four-Block, Four-Semester Program

In Block I of the program (fall semester, junior year), the content focuses on foundations and preschool curriculum, with our juniors spending time in preschool settings. These settings include both public and private agencies that allow the preservice teachers to interact with children ages two to five.

In Block II of the program (spring semester, junior year), each preservice teacher is placed with a mentor teacher for approximately one and a half days per week. The mentors are kindergarten, first-grade, or kindergarten/first-grade teachers. Preservice teachers spend Blocks II, III, and IV (totaling one and a half school years) with the same mentor. The children in the classrooms change in Block III (fall semester, senior year) because it is a new school year, but the preservice teacher stays with the same mentor. In the spring of each year, the classrooms have both a Block II and a Block IV preservice teacher. The organization of the program provides two mentors for each preservice teacher in Block II: an experienced certified teacher and a senior preservice teacher in Block IV. In this way, our program strives to provide a supervised apprenticeship for our students. The Block II student has two mentors who work with him or her in the classroom setting, providing emotional and curricular support.

In Blocks II and III, preservice teachers create thematic units and teach them under the guidance of their mentor teacher and university supervisor. In Block II, preservice teachers design and implement a one-week unit and spend a week in April as the lead teacher in their classrooms. For this week, their university classes are excused. In Block III, preservice teachers design and implement a two-week unit on a different topic and are released from their university classes for two weeks in November.

Block IV (spring semester, senior year) involves what is traditionally referred to as "student teaching." However, instead of having a brief stint of student teaching, our students are in their third semester with the same mentor, which creates a fluid co-teaching enterprise. The three blocks spent in the field with the same mentor offer students opportunities for cognitive and intellectual growth, and the mentor and university supervisor implement specific strategies with each student targeting his or her zone of proximal development.

Integrating Service Learning with Course Work

The long-term commitment we have with mentors and schools allows us to integrate service learning into our program with their support. Integration begins in Block I, where the preservice teachers work with the homeless coalition to implement service learning in the community. Undergraduate students are taught the pedagogy of service learning and learn how service learning connects with early childhood education. In Block II, service learning is infused in two linked courses—Early Childhood Curriculum and Methods and the field course Methods and Early Childhood Observation and Participation (a two-day-a-week practicum in one of the local elementary schools in a preK to third-grade classroom. These preservice teachers are then tasked with designing and implementing a service learning project that emerges from their curriculum for the children in their field placement classroom. Over the course of the semester, which includes a one-week full-time teaching period in April, preservice teachers create a thematic unit that includes the service learning project. Many of them plan their projects together, and several schools often do the same project. At the end of the semester, the undergraduate students submit their service learning plan along with two evaluations—one completed by them and one completed with their elementary students—to the course instructors.

The following fall, Block III includes five methods courses and the practicum course. These courses are required for the preservice teachers' professional development sequence and provide them with their third long-term fieldwork placement. Our undergraduate students are aware of the focus on and commitment to the integration of service learning and early childhood curriculum through the syllabi, discussions, and joint assignments. Service learning ideas, concepts, and knowledge are infused in the mathematics, science, and social studies methods courses, as well as in the observation and participation course.

Service Learning Project Varieties

Judging from the outcomes and evaluations from our initial year of the program, the variety of projects was a huge success and, for most of our

> The variety of projects was a huge success and, for most of our preservice teachers and their children, service learning was one of the highlights of their teaching units.

preservice teachers and their children, service learning was one of the highlights of their teaching units. Many of the preservice teachers planned the projects and worked together by school location. The first year's projects fell into four main categories: environmental awareness, gardening, letter writing, and helping people in need. (See the chart on page 195.)

Subsequent projects in the following years have yielded similar types of projects. Most service learning projects emerge from the preservice teachers' field placement curriculum and often correlate with the time of year. Many spring projects centered on gardening and pollution, while the fall projects were influenced by Thanksgiving concepts and environmental awareness. One year, almost half of the fall projects were designed to provide relief for victims of four hurricanes that hit Florida. Ten classrooms participated in canned food drives and/or hurricane relief. Preservice teachers in one school approached the principal about having kindergartners share their service learning project with the whole school via the morning news show; the project soon turned into a school-wide effort with two truckloads of materials and over $900 raised for schools in Pensacola, Florida.

Many letter writing projects also take place each semester. Some projects involve advocacy, such as writing letters to the state's governor to protect marine life. Some projects are letters and cards sent to support U.S. troops, to thank area farmers, or to reach out to elderly residents. No matter what the focus, all of the projects demonstrate the empowering nature of service learning with young children and teachers by connecting them to their communities through curriculum-based projects. Each semester of our program, more than 525 preK through third-grade children are involved in service learning projects designed and implemented by the early childhood preservice teachers.

Preservice Teacher and Child Evaluations

At the end of each semester, participants in our program provide us with copies of their thematic teaching units and service learning plans. They also provide artifacts from their service learning projects, including photographs, samples of student work, posters, and activity logs. Initially, the preservice teachers and preK through third-grade students were also administered a four-part evaluation that asked the following questions: *What happened? How do I feel? Ideas?* and *Questions?* However, the questions proved too vague for many young children. Therefore, preservice teachers now respond in writing to 12 questions that target the effectiveness of their project, concepts and skills taught, children's academic and social benefits of participating in the project, how the project supported the state standards, and specific products of their projects. (See **Teacher Assessment of the Service Learning Project** on pages 113–114).

Qualitative data is also collected from the children via a series of six questions (See

Child-to-Child Evaluation of Service Learning on pages 104–105.) Several children are randomly selected to answer the following questions asked by a preservice teacher or known adult:

1. Tell me about your service learning project.
2. What did you learn from this project that you didn't know before?
3. How was your project helpful?
4. How did your project help other people, animals, or the environment?
5. What other things have you done to be helpful since working on your project?
6. How did working on this project compare to the rest of your schoolwork?

Preservice Teacher Responses
How Effective and Beneficial Was This Project?

The preservice teachers were asked the following questions about their project:

- How effective was the service learning project?

Service Learning Projects by Category

Category	Projects
Environmental Awareness	Adopt a Turtle or Manatee Give a Hoot, Don't Pollute! Recycling in the Classroom and School Environmental Cleanup Projects Making Bird Feeders Bat Posters and Awareness Recycled Art
Gardening	Mother's/Father's Day School Beautification Planet Beautification
Letter Writing	Letters to Troops Letters to Local Veterans Letters to Elderly Letters to Government Officials Letters to Family Letters to Other Classes Letters to Farmers
Helping People in Need	Canned Food Drives Hurricane Relief Efforts Totes for Kids in Hospitals

- How did the children benefit from participating in the project?

The teachers who conducted the advocacy rainforest projects reported an appreciation for the rainforest and its products (fruits, spices, medicine) by their children. Preservice teachers also discussed a sense of empowerment discovered by their children:

> "They feel like if there is a problem in the world then they have the power to do something about it. It gave them a deeper understanding of how people influence each other." —*Carol*

The canned food drives were successful for most of the preservice teachers. They all focused on community members who were less fortunate, the process of giving to people in need, and how young children are able to contribute to their community. A few children, on their own, classified the cans in different ways, which was one of the math skills for this project. The kindergarten class was taught about cancer and wrote to children with cancer. As one teacher stated:

> "They thought of other children who were struggling with something that they could barely fathom. It made the children think outside of themselves." —*Keith*

However, not all the service learning projects were considered successful, as another teacher describes:

> "[The project] could have been more effective. During the lesson many of the kids had trouble staying on task, so when it came time to write their letters, the children had problems thinking of reasons why you should recycle, even though we went over a dozen specific reasons during the lesson." —*Megan*

The majority of the preservice teachers, however, stated that their service learning projects had been effective; only two preservice teachers in these two years suggested that their projects were not successful.

What Changes Have Occurred in Your Students?

The preservice teachers were also asked the following questions with regards to their students:

- What changes in students' knowledge and performance have occurred as a result of the project?
- What changes in students' attitudes and behavior have occurred as a result of the project?
- What changes in students' enthusiasm or motivation have occurred as a result of the project?

Few preservice teachers reported no change in the children in their classrooms as a result of participating in the service learning projects. Preservice teachers who conducted indirect letter writing service learning projects noted that some children were more expressive in their journal writing than before the project, but that, as a class, they did not observe any overt changes in their children. Although it is very difficult to definitively connect changes in children to the service learning projects, the following examples do directly tie to the concepts taught by the preservice teacher and cooperating teacher; the children were not exhibiting these behaviors before the service learning projects.

The preservice teachers who concentrated on hurricane and natural disaster relief reported that the children began to listen to the news more in order to track hurricanes and other natural disasters. This led to more discussion of hurricanes in the classroom and on the playground, and hurricane and disaster play became more prevalent. In one classroom, the children requested that the preservice and cooperating teacher only read "true story" books (stories about real people), because they said these books reminded them of how much they helped others.

As a result of the canned food drive service learning projects, the preservice teachers noticed that the children were much more aware of what they ate in the classroom:

> "They don't like throwing away food. I feel that they have become more conscientious of the things they have and how others don't have as much as they do." —*Elena*

> "[They are] not complaining about how much they get for snack." —*Keesha*

After completing the rainforest project that focused on recycling and writing the governor, the children were very motivated to pick up every piece of paper in the classroom and recycle it. One preservice teacher remarked that her children used the governor's name a lot more since writing to him:

> "Whenever something needs to be done about anything, the students want me to ask the governor to help or they want to write him again." —*Noel*

Will You Use Service Learning in Your Own Instruction?

Every preservice teacher said that she or he was planning to use service learning in her or his own instruction. A few said they wanted to teach a few years first and then implement service learning. All groups of teachers discussed that service learning was now a natural part of their teaching. One teacher responded:

> "[Children need to be] engaged in hands-on experiences that help them grow as human beings." —*Maria*

What Have Been Barriers to Your Service Learning Project?

Preservice teachers listed *expense* as a major barrier to the service learning projects. Either the teacher used his or her own money; it was difficult to raise money for the project; or he or she did not know how to handle the inequity of the money or goods the children brought in. In all cases, the cooperating teacher guided and helped the novice teacher.

Another barrier mentioned was the *lack of parental support* for the projects. About one-third of each teacher group invited parents to the classroom for the documentation portion of the project, and there was no written evidence that any parent was present.

Another barrier mentioned by preservice teachers at three of the schools was that some of the *children had a difficult time with the concept of "people in need."* The teachers attributed this difficulty to the affluence of the neighborhoods and schools involved and the children's lack of exposure to those less fortunate than them.

The last barrier commonly mentioned was *lack of time:*

> "There are so many restrictions to students in the public school classroom that I found it hard to squeeze [service learning] in there while everything else still needed to be done." —*Jenna*

A Note About Open Court and Similar Programs

Several teachers stated that they did not have enough time to do service learning because of the amount of time spent on Open Court and worksheets. Open Court is a widely used elementary-level reading and English language arts curriculum program that is considered an "intensive intervention" model in No Child Left Behind (NCLB) and as an overall curriculum according to DAP guidelines. In our district, some early childhood teachers are spending up to two-and-a-half hours a day in their Open Court block. Curriculum in a model such as Open Court is grounded in systematic, explicit instruction, and often is not integrated, experiential, or constructivist in nature. Therefore, most of our preservice teachers would not have been allowed to even teach their service learning projects if they had *not* been called "service learning." If the recycling, letter writing, gardening, or pollution service learning projects had instead been labeled as "hands-on projects," "conceptual learning projects," or "interactive learning projects," we doubt that time would have been made for them or that they would have been approved to be taught at all. In classrooms that have moved so far toward skills-based instruction and further away from practices that integrate curriculum, service learning can be a way of introducing, maintaining, or keeping appropriate practices for young children in classrooms.

4

While the findings just reported highlight the effectiveness of the service learning projects, information from the preK to third-grade students is needed to fully evaluate the projects. In our study, this was accomplished by having the children orally respond to several questions.

Children's Responses

Each preservice teacher gathered the children's evaluations from a classroom in the school other than her or his own. This design allowed the teacher who was interviewing the children to assume the researcher friend role versus the authoritative teacher role. However, for every question asked about the projects, several children answered, "I don't know." Henceforth, the following sections of children's responses will not include that response.

Tell Me About Your Service Learning Project

The children's responses to the canned food drive projects elicited several answers that focused on the process of the project:

> "We cut out hands and said what we were thankful for. Everybody brought in a lot of food and put them in a bag. We wrote letters to give to the people about what we are thankful for."

> "We brought cans of food for people that don't have food."

The rainforest letter writing campaign yielded more factual responses, such as:

> "We get oxygen from trees."

> "We get medicine and food from the rainforest."

> "I didn't know paper was made from trees."

> "I didn't know that we were killing the animals of the rainforest and selling them as pets."

> "I didn't know there were over 300 different birds in the rainforest."

Children whose projects concentrated on cancer outreach answered the prompt from a more emotional standpoint:

> "I learned that people with cancer are very sick and need help from other people to make them feel better."

> "I learned about helping people feel better."

> "[I learned about] helping others and not always caring just about me."

How Has Your Project Been Helpful?

One child who wrote a letter to veterans responded:

> "It was a nice thing to do for people who take care of us."

Several children stated that they did not know their dads were veterans until they told them about the service learning project, thus demonstrating the home connection. These children made an additional card or letter for their fathers.

Canned food drives were popular for natural disasters, homelessness, and the Thanksgiving holiday, and children responded to the question by citing personal experience and by generalizing the need for food drives. Responses included:

> "Because of the tornado where Suzy is, we had to bring food for them because it was fast and we had to help them."

> "If they don't get food they are going to die. I just know that."

> "We were nice and gave them food. If we didn't, they wouldn't have anything for dinner or breakfast."

Responses from the recycling projects were more skill-oriented:

> "It taught us that it is good to recycle so you have less garbage."

> "It was a good thing because now I know how I can help the environment."

When asked how they were being helpful since completing their service learning projects, the majority of the preservice teachers received specific responses from the children they interviewed:

- After food drive projects: "I have been eating at home, salad, broccoli, green beans. So I can grow big and strong."

- After gardening projects: "You gotta be nice to people. If people are nice to you, you give something to them."

- After hospital patient outreach projects: "I helped a friend. When Jessica falls, I help her get off the ground."

- After letter writing projects: "I care about people, because if they get hurt I just help them up because all the people need caring and love."

- After hurricane relief projects: "I gave some of my toys away." "I shared with my brother."

In addition, almost all the children who did recycling projects talked about recycling paper in their classrooms and at home when asked what they were doing to be helpful since finishing their projects.

Making Sense of the Preservice Teachers' and Children's Responses

Several major findings emerged from our program's service learning projects and evaluations over several years that illustrate the theory and concepts in this book. The first was that integrating early childhood teacher education curriculum and service learning created a teaching space for experiential learning and developmentally appropriate practices in classrooms that, due to curricular constraints, are moving further away from these instructional approaches. A second finding that emerged is that service learning projects are a vehicle for empowerment in young children. Furthermore, service learning is not separate from the state or national standards and should not be thought of as separate or as an "add-on" to the regular curriculum. Finally, the service learning projects provided the preservice teachers with meaningful learning opportunities, and infusing service learning into teacher education proved to be an avenue for teaching in a constructivist, integrated manner.

Service Learning and Children's Literature

The following section describes how our teacher education program used the course on children's literature to expand the pedagogy of service learning and demonstrate to the preservice teachers how children's books can be the impetus for classroom service learning projects. As a teacher or teacher educator, you know that children who are good readers often love to read. Knowing how to choose literature, which methods of instruction use literature and story elements, and what extension activities tap into a variety of learning styles and multiple intelligences are just some of the hallmarks of a good children's literature course in a teacher education program. However, literature can also be used as the springboard for service learning.

> Children's books provide children with information, inspire them to consider important topics, and give them a range of possibilities for their own actions.

Preservice and in-service teachers are taught how literature enriches the personal lives of children. Children's books enable readers to see the world around them with new eyes and consider ways of living other than their own. Children may develop a greater capacity to empathize with others by walking in their shoes. Children's literature courses can help students understand that children's books provide children with information, inspire them to consider important topics, and give them a range of possibilities for their own actions. Books can serve as catalysts for action by leading children to consider many questions, such as: What actions are making a difference in the lives of others? Are any of the problems or conflicts in the story occurring in my life or the lives of people I know or see? What can we do to address problems in our community that are similar to the ones described in the book?[6]

Children's literature titles can also serve as engaging focal points for discussions of service learning in your PLC.

Sample Service Learning Projects Using Children's Literature

In our program, early childhood education students worked in five cooperative groups during class with scaffolded support from the professor and outside of class to prepare a service learning project for elementary students with literature serving as a core element in their plans. Using Cathryn Berger Kaye's book, *The Complete Guide to Service Learning*, as a guide, the students chose the theme as well as the type of project—direct service, indirect service, advocacy, or research. Project themes included animals in danger, the environment, gardening, hunger and homelessness, and immigrants. Each plan included quality children's literature and utilized the following four stages of service learning— preparation, action, reflection, and documentation.

Theme: Animals in Danger

The needs addressed for animals in danger were those of the loggerhead turtles. To introduce the unit to kindergartners and create the need to "Save the Loggerheads," the book *Follow That Fish* by Joanne Oppenheim was read aloud to illustrate the precarious existence of sea creatures. Further information of the plight was gained from *Interrupted Journey: Saving Endangered Sea Turtles* by Kathryn Lasky. This book was read to the students before their field trip to St. Andrew's State Park, where the park ranger gave an age-appropriate presentation on the loggerhead turtle restoration and protection project. During this advocacy unit, a class learning center entitled "Sea" was stocked with 17 picture books on the subject that helped students gather even more information.

Reflection and documentation for this topic included a play for the kindergarten families that consisted of several children acting as rangers presenting a brief statement and other children acting out their parts. The children modeled the behavior of tourists, fishermen, and boaters and how their behavior negatively affects the turtles. Then, other children acted out good citizen behavior that is helpful to the turtles. After the play, a snack was shared with the families, and the children modeled proper disposal of trash when the snack was finished.

Theme: The Environment

In another advocacy project involving the environment, elementary students observed the difference between degradable and nondegradable waste materials in mini-landfills. The third- and fourth-grade students listened to *The Magic School Bus Meets the Rot Squad: A Book About Decomposition* as they began looking at garbage in different ways to reduce the amount of material that is dumped in landfills. The classes then observed the difference between degradable and nondegradable waste materials stored in glass and plastic jars throughout the room. A field trip to the local dump was included in this project. Action, reflection, and documentation took place as the students built a compost bin for their school and educated the rest of the school about their new bin.

Theme: Gardening

The gardening project was introduced by reading *The Gardener* by Sarah Stewart aloud to prekindergarten and kindergarten students. This book illustrated the joy that flowers can bring to others. During this service learning activity, young children planted a flower garden with the help of the high school club, Future Farmers of America, and the local garden club. *The Gardener* was instrumental in promoting caring for others and opened the door to students' enjoyment and commitment to helping the sick and elderly. Reflection and documentation occurred in the culminating activity in which children delivered flowers to the residents of a nursing home.

Theme: Hunger and Homelessness

The faces of homelessness were no longer invisible to the elementary students participating in a service learning project after listening to two poignant books written by Eve Bunting: *Fly Away Home* and *Train to Somewhere*. Before collecting and delivering blankets to homeless shelters, elementary students discussed the following questions during their project: Who is homeless? Why are they homeless? What can we do to help people who are homeless? What can we do to reduce or eliminate

---

[6] Kaye (2010), p. 53

homelessness? Throughout this project, the children reflected on homelessness and hunger through illustrations and group murals, poetry, and a class book that highlighted individual journal entries. These project artifacts were then shared with other classes.

Theme: Immigrants

This project sought to raise children's awareness of the plight of migrant families by planning a research service learning project. The teacher read aloud Francisco Jiménez's *The Circuit: Stories from the Life of a Migrant Child,* which illustrated life in a migrant camp for students. The focus of this project was to research available community services that support migrant children and families. The students reflected on their project by creating a mural comparing their lives to those of migrant children. Brochures that had been collected from the various service agencies were disseminated.

As these five projects demonstrate, integrating service learning pedagogy with existing course reading and assignments actually enhances, versus detracts from, the course content. In fact, many early childhood classrooms across the nation are implementing service learning projects, but they do not know that what they are doing is called service learning. In our classes, we heard this over and over again. The preservice and in-service teachers explained that they were already doing many projects that with a little tweaking—adding the reflection and documentation pieces—they could label as service learning.

You may also find this to be true in your PLC: many teachers are already doing service learning,

and some seasoned teachers have been doing it for years, without knowing it. Start a discussion among your colleagues about how you integrate course reading with hands-on learning. You may be surprised just how common service learning is in your school community, and how readily it can be harnessed and its benefits multiplied.

> *Note:* See pages 205–207 for children's book recomendations that correspond to the sample lesson plans in Part Three.

Chapter Summary

Integrating service learning into the curriculum of a teacher education program or PLC discussion is not an end in itself, but a means of achieving basic educational goals. In addition, the opportunity to learn about service learning, as well as to engage in service learning at different levels, empowers teachers as well as the young children they work with. Best practices in early childhood curriculum call for active, hands-on learning; cooperative learning; integrated curriculum; and meaningful, relevant learning experiences, among others. The cascading model of integrating early childhood curriculum and service learning outlines these best practices for preservice teachers and teacher education programs. Both the cascading and children's literature models are avenues that colleges and universities can implement to improve the quality of teaching, as well as respond to the call to return to their historic service commitment.

K–12 Service Learning Standards and Indicators for Quality Practice[1]

Meaningful Service

Service learning actively engages participants in meaningful and personally relevant service activities.

Indicators:

1. Service learning experiences are appropriate to participant ages and developmental abilities.
2. Service learning addresses issues that are personally relevant to the participants.
3. Service learning provides participants with interesting and engaging service activities.
4. Service learning encourages participants to understand their service experiences in the context of the underlying societal issues being addressed.
5. Service learning leads to attainable and visible outcomes that are valued by those being served.

Link to Curriculum

Service learning is intentionally used as an instructional strategy to meet learning goals and/or content standards.

Indicators:

1. Service learning has clearly articulated learning goals.
2. Service learning is aligned with the academic and/or programmatic curriculum.
3. Service learning helps participants learn how to transfer knowledge and skills from one setting to another.
4. Service learning that takes place in schools is formally recognized in school board policies and student records.

Reflection

Service learning incorporates multiple challenging reflection activities that are ongoing and that prompt deep thinking and analysis about oneself and one's relationship to society.

Indicators:

1. Service learning reflection includes a variety of verbal, written, artistic, and nonverbal activities to demonstrate understanding and changes in participants' knowledge, skills, and/or attitudes.
2. Service learning reflection occurs before, during, and after the service experience.
3. Service learning reflection prompts participants to think deeply about complex community problems and alternative solutions.
4. Service learning reflection encourages participants to examine their preconceptions and assumptions in order to explore and understand their roles and responsibilities as citizens.
5. Service learning reflection encourages participants to examine a variety of social and civic issues related to their service learning experience so that participants understand connections to public policy and civic life.

Diversity

Service learning promotes understanding of diversity and mutual respect among all participants.

Indicators:

1. Service learning helps participants identify and analyze different points of view to gain understanding of multiple perspectives.

---

[1] National Youth Leadership Council (2008), www.nylc.org. Reprinted with permission.

2. Service learning helps participants develop interpersonal skills in conflict resolution and group decision making.

3. Service learning helps participants actively seek to understand and value the diverse backgrounds and perspectives of those offering and receiving service.

4. Service learning encourages participants to recognize and overcome stereotypes.

Youth Voice

Service learning provides youth with a strong voice in planning, implementing, and evaluating service learning experiences with guidance from adults.
   Indicators:

1. Service learning engages youth in generating ideas during the planning, implementation, and evaluation processes.

2. Service learning involves youth in the decision-making process throughout the service learning experiences.

3. Service learning involves youth and adults in creating an environment that supports trust and open expression of ideas.

4. Service learning promotes acquisition of knowledge and skills to enhance youth leadership and decision making.

5. Service learning involves youth in evaluating the quality and effectiveness of the service learning experience.

Partnerships

Service learning partnerships are collaborative, mutually beneficial, and address community needs.
   Indicators:

1. Service learning involves a variety of partners, including youth, educators, families, community members, community-based organizations, and/or businesses.

2. Service learning partnerships are characterized by frequent and regular communication to keep all partners well informed about activities and progress.

3. Service learning partners collaborate to establish a shared vision and set common goals to address community needs.

4. Service learning partners collaboratively develop and implement action plans to meet specified goals.

5. Service learning partners share knowledge and understanding of school and community assets and needs, and view each other as valued resources.

Progress Monitoring

Service learning engages participants in an ongoing process to assess the quality of implementation and progress toward meeting specified goals, and uses results for improvement and sustainability.
   Indicators:

1. Service learning participants collect evidence of progress toward meeting specific service goals and learning outcomes from multiple sources throughout the service learning experience.

2. Service learning participants collect evidence of the quality of service learning implementation from multiple sources throughout the service learning experience.

3. Service learning participants use evidence to improve service learning experiences.

4. Service learning participants communicate evidence of progress toward goals and outcomes with the broader community, including policymakers and education leaders, to deepen service learning understanding and ensure that high-quality practices are sustained.

Duration and Intensity

Service learning has sufficient duration and intensity to address community needs and meet specified outcomes.
   Indicators:

1. Service learning experiences include the processes of investigating community needs, preparing for service, action, reflection, demonstration of learning and impacts, and celebration.

2. Service learning is conducted during concentrated blocks of time across a period of several weeks or months.

3. Service learning experiences provide enough time to address identified community needs and achieve learning outcomes

Resources

Chapter 1

Corporation for National and Community Service (CNCS)
nationalservice.gov
Like the Corporation for Public Broadcasting, CNCS is a public, nonprofit corporation funded through federal appropriation. It is the nation's largest grant maker supporting service and volunteering. Through its Senior Corps, AmeriCorps, and Learn and Serve America programs, CNCS provides opportunities for Americans of all ages and backgrounds to express their patriotism while addressing critical community needs.

National Service Learning Clearinghouse (NSLC)
servicelearning.org
NSLC is funded by the Corporation for National and Community Service. It supports the service learning community in higher education, K–12, community-based initiatives and tribal programs, as well as all others interested in strengthening schools and communities using service learning techniques and methodologies with materials, references, referrals, and other information.

National Service Learning Partnership
servicelearningpartnership.org
The Partnership, founded in 2001, is a national network of members dedicated to advancing service learning as a core part of every young person's education. The Partnership concentrates on strengthening the impact of service learning on young people's learning and development, especially their academic and civic preparation. The Partnership supports members sharing resources, organizing change, and sponsoring innovation.

National Society for Experiential Education (NSEE)
nsee.org
NSEE is a nonprofit membership association of educators, businesses, and community leaders. Founded in 1971, NSEE also serves as a national resource center for the development and improvement of experiential education programs nationwide. NSEE supports the use of learning through experience for intellectual development, cross-cultural and global awareness, civic and social responsibility, ethical development, career exploration, and personal growth.

National Youth Leadership Council (NYLC)
nylc.org
For more than 25 years NYLC has led a movement that links kids, educators, and communities to redefine the roles of young people in society. Its website includes a wealth of resources and up-to-date information about service learning.

Chapter 2

The Center for the 4th and 5th Rs
www2.cortland.edu/centers/character
The Center for the 4th and 5th Rs conducts K–12 character education trainings, research, and evaluation and publishes *The Fourth and Fifth Rs* "best practices" newsletter. The center defines character education as the intentional integration of excellence and ethics—developing performance character (doing our best work) and moral character (doing the right thing) within an ethical learning community.

Character Counts
charactercounts.org
The Josephson Institute Center for Youth Ethics, a nonprofit organization, administers the national office of Character Counts, the largest and most widely implemented character education program in the United States.

Funderstanding
funderstanding.com
This site provides user- and kid-friendly information on many kinds of information, including Piaget, Vygotsky, constructivist theories, and more.

Learn and Serve America (LSA)
learnandserve.gov
A program of the Corporation for National and Community Service, LSA supports and encourages service learning throughout the United States and enables over one million students to make meaningful contributions to their community while building their academic and civic skills. LSA provides direct and indirect support to K–12 schools, community groups, and higher education institutions to facilitate service learning projects.

Chapter 3

Common Core State Standards Initiative (CCSSI)
corestandards.org
CCSSI is a state-led effort coordinated by the National Governors Association Center for Best Practices (NGA Center) and the Council of Chief State School Officers (CCSSO). The standards were developed in collaboration with teachers, school administrators, and experts, to provide a clear and consistent framework to prepare our children for college and the workforce.

Learning to Give
learningtogive.org
Learning to Give educates kids about the importance of philanthropy, the civil society sector, and civic engagement. The Learning to Give website offers over 1,200 K–12 lessons and educational resources for teachers, parents, youth workers, faith groups, and community leaders, free of charge.

Teaching for Change
teachingforchange.org
Teaching for Change, established in 1989, operates from the belief that schools can provide students the skills, knowledge, and inspiration to be citizens and architects of a better world. By drawing direct connections to real-world issues, Teaching for Change encourages teachers and students to question and rethink the world inside and outside their classrooms; build a more equitable, multicultural society; and become active global citizens.

Chapter 4

Campus Compact

compact.org/syllabi

In this section of the Campus Compact site, you will find over 300 exemplary service learning syllabi across a wide variety of disciplines. The introduction provides a framework by which educators can best conceptualize integrating service learning into their courses.

National Center for Learning and Citizenship (NCLC)

ecs.org/nclc

NCLC is an organization of chief state school officers, district superintendents, service learning professionals, and others who support service learning. Members are committed to linking school-based service and service learning to K–12 curriculum and to organizing schools to maximize community volunteer efforts. This site contains publications, resources, related links, and information about membership.

National Service Learning Clearinghouse: Service Learning Ideas and Curricular Examples (SLICE)

servicelearning.org/slice

This section of the NSLC site contains K–12 lesson plans that are searchable and broken down by theme. Click on the theme to read a one- to two-sentence description.

New Horizons for Learning

education.jhu.edu/newhorizons

New Horizons for Learning, a resource from the Johns Hopkins University School of Education, provides visibility to effective teaching and learning practices and ideas that have not yet reached the mainstream. Search for "service learning" for information and related articles.

Students in Service to America

studentsinservice.org

Peruse the collection of resources for novice and experienced service learning users.

Chapter 9

Education World

education-world.com

This site is very useful if you plan to have your students write letters as part of their service learning project. You'll find ideas for topics as well as information about pairing students around the world with pen pals.

Hedgie's Home Page

janbrett.com/stationery/friendly_stationery_main.htm

Are your students writing letters as part of their service learning project? Download fun, printable stationery from this site in both black-and-white and color. There are also four interactive templates students can use to type their letters; they can then print them from the site.

Letters to Soldiers.Org

letterstosoldiers.org

This website expresses the importance of writing to deployed troops and has several examples of letters to soldiers. Though the letters on the site have not been written by children, they will give your students some ideas they can incorporate into their own letters. Students can send their letters via the email address provided on the site, which ensures that their letters will be directly delivered to soldiers stationed overseas.

Soldiers' Angels

soldiersangels.org

This amazing organization is dedicated to not letting any soldier go unloved. A class, grade, or school can adopt a soldier and send one letter every week, as well as one or two packages a month.

U.S. Department of Agriculture Kids' Zone

agclassroom.org/kids/index.htm

Find answers to some commonly asked questions about agriculture and farming, which can be used as part of an introductory activity to a unit on farming.

Write On Project

jc-schools.net/write/letter-write.htm

With examples of appropriate letters, this site from Jefferson County Schools in Tennessee can help your students learn how to write and reach many different people, including the president, Congress, and international pen pals. It offers advice and specific topics to focus on and provides a rubric for each type of letter.

Caillou Sends a Letter by Joceline Sanschagrin. Montreal, Quebec: Chouette Publishing, 2008.

Captain Cat by Syd Hoff. New York: HarperCollins Publishers, 1994.

Corduroy Writes a Letter by Alison Inches, et al. New York: Penguin Group USA, 2004.

Farming by Gail Gibbons. New York: Holiday House, 1988.

Hero Dad by Melinda Hardin. Tarrytown, NY: Marshall Cavendish Children's Books, 2010.

Hold the Flag High by Catherine Clinton and Shane W. Evans. New York: Katherine Tegen Books, 2005.

I Wanna Iguana by Karen Kaufman Orloff. New York: Putnam, 2004.

Messages in the Mailbox: How to Write a Letter by Loreen Leedy. New York: Holiday House, 1991.

Nature's Green Umbrella: Tropical Rain Forests by Gail Gibbons. New York: Morrow Junior Books, 1994.

Putting It in Writing by Steve Otfinoski. New York: Scholastic Guides, 1994.

The Farmer by Mark Ludy. Windsor, CO: Green Pastures Publishing, 1999.

The Jolly Postman, or, Other People's Letters by Allan and Janet Ahlberg. New York: LB-Kids, 2006.

The Vanishing Rainforest by Richard Platt and illustrated by Rupert van Wyk. London: Frances Lincoln Children's Books, 2004.

Welcome to the Green House by Jane Yolen. New York: Putnam, 1993.

While You Are Away by Eileen Spinelli. New York: Hyperion, 2008.

Chapter 10

EcoKids
ecokids.ca
The EcoKids site is divided into two user-friendly sections, one for kids and one for teachers. EcoKids clean and plant to beautify the earth, and if your students want to be EcoKids, too, the site has information on how to join, as well as lots of photos.

KidsGardening
kidsgardening.org
Browse the KidsGardening online store, where you can purchase many kinds of books, seeds, and other materials. Get tips on keeping a green thumb and landscaping. The site also announces fundraisers and partner projects for international cooperative learning.

Care Bears: How Does Your Garden Grow? by Frances Ann Ladd. New York: Scholastic, 2004.

City Green by DyAnne DiSalvo-Ryan. New York: Morrow Junior Books, 1994.

Dig, Plant, Grow: A Kid's Guide to Gardening by Felder Rushing. Nashville, TN: Cool Springs Press, 2004.

Digging Deeper: Integrating Youth Gardens into Schools and Communities by Joseph Kiefer and Martin Kemple. Montpelier, VT: Common Roots Press, 1998.

Flower Garden by Eve Bunting. Orlando, FL: Red Wagon Books/ Harcourt, 2008.

From Seed to Plant by Gail Gibbons. New York: Holiday House, 1993.

Gardening with Children by Monika Hanneman. Brooklyn, NY: Brooklyn Botanic Garden, 2011.

Greening School Grounds by Tim Grant and Gail Littlejohn. Gabriola Island, BC: New Society Publishers, 2001.

Holly Bloom's Garden by Sarah Ashman. Brooklyn, NY: Flashlight Press, 2008.

How Groundhog's Garden Grew by Lynne Cherry. New York: Blue Sky Press, 2003.

Jack's Garden by Henry Cole. New York: HarperCollins Publishers, 1997.

Ms. Spitzer's Garden by Edith Pattou. New York: Harcourt Children's Books, 2007.

Roots, Shoots, Buckets, and Boots: Gardening Together with Children by Sharon Lovejoy. New York: Workman Publishing, 1999.

The Gardening Book by Jane Bull. New York: DK Publishing, 2003.

The Growing Garden: Garden-Based Science by Roberta Jaffe and Gary Appel. South Burlington, VT: National Gardening Association, 2007.

Whose Garden Is It? by Mary Ann Hobberman. New York: Harcourt Children's Books, 2004.

Chapter 11

Feeding America
feedingamerica.org
This website provides information about hunger in the United States, and what Feeding America is doing to help relieve it. You can also find a local food bank where you and your students can donate food.

Just Neighbors
justneighbors.net
Just Neighbors is an organization that aims to raise awareness of the root causes of poverty and homelessness. You can order a toolkit that contains materials for conducting several lessons on poverty and homelessness. Although the program is intended for adolescents, parts of it could be adapted to be used with young children.

Ready Kids
ready.gov/kids
This website has a lot of kid-friendly information about disasters and emergencies, including how to prepare for one.

A Shelter in Our Car by Monica Gunning. San Francisco: Children's Book Press, 2004.

Clifford and the Big Storm by Norman Bridwell. New York: Scholastic Press, 1995.

Cooper's Tale by Ralph da Costa Nunez. New York: Homes for the Homeless Inc., 2000.

Do Tornadoes Really Twist? Questions and Answers About Tornadoes and Hurricanes by Melvin and Gilda Berger. New York: Scholastic, 2000.

Eye of the Storm: A Book About Hurricanes by Rick Thomas. Minneapolis, MN: Picture Window Books, 2003.

Fly Away Home by Eve Bunting. New York: Clarion Books, 1991.

Gowanus Dogs by Jonathan Frost. New York: Farrar, Straus and Giroux, 1999.

Hurricane by David Wiesner. New York: Sandpiper, 2008.

Let's Talk About Staying in a Shelter by Elizabeth Weitzman. New York: PowerKids Press, 2003.

Rosie: The Shopping Cart Lady by Chia Martin. Prescott, AZ: Hohm Press, 1996.

Sergio and the Hurricane by Alexandra Wallner. New York: Henry Holt and Co., 2000.

Someplace to Go by Maria Testa. Morton Grove, IL: Albert Whitman and Company, 1996.

Stone Soup by Ann McGovern. New York: Scholastic, 1986.

The Berenstain Bears Think of Those in Need by Stan and Jan Berenstain. New York: Random House Books for Young Readers, 1999.

The Lady in the Box by Ann McGovern. New York: Turtle Books, 1997.

The Teddy Bear by David McPhail. New York: Henry Holt and Company, 2002.

Uncle Willie and the Soup Kitchen by Dyanne Disalvo-Ryan. New York: HarperCollins, 1997.

Chapter 12

Endangered Specie
endangeredspecie.com
This site has a lot of information about endangered species. Kids can find out what species are endangered in their state, why it's important to save them, causes of endangerment, the definitions of *vulnerable*, *threatened*, *endangered*, and *extinct*, and some simple ways to help. There is also a very large bookstore including a variety of books about endangered species.

EPA Students
epa.gov/students
This kids' corner of the Environmental Protection Agency includes games, homework resources, community service projects, summer programs, teacher resources, awards and contests, Earth Day information, and much more.

Kids Recycle!
kidsrecycle.org/index.php
This website is easily accessible to teachers and students, designed to help achieve zero waste in the school system. Students are encouraged to make their own posters and contribute them to the site, and they can also share links to songs about recycling. If kids' recycling efforts have made the local news, they can send the information along and it will be posted to the site.

Recycle City
epa.gov/recyclecity
Recycle City is big enough for kids *and* grown-ups. Teachers can learn how to use Recycle City in their classroom, and kids can use their gaming skills to turn Dumptown into Recycle City.

An Elephant in the Backyard by Richard Sobol. New York: Dutton Children's Books, 2004.

Awesome Things to Make with Recycled Stuff by Joe Rhatigan and Heather Smith. New York: Lark Books, 2003.

Dancing with Manatees (Hello Reader! Series) by Faith McNulty. New York: Scholastic Press, 1998.

Earthsong by Sally Rogers. New York: Dutton Children's Books, 1998.

Eyewitness: Endangered Animals by Ben Hoare. New York: DK Publishing, 2010.

Help the Animals of Africa by Robert Sabuda. New York: Readers Digest Association, 1995.

I Wonder Why the Dodo Is Dead: And Other Questions About Extinct and Endangered Animals by Andrew Charman. Boston: Kingfisher, 2007.

I'm a Manatee by John Lithgow. New York: Simon & Schuster Books for Young Readers, 2003.

Jaguarundi by Virginia Hamilton. New York: Blue Sky Press, 1997.

Let's Recycle by Claire Llewelyn. North Mankato, MN: Chrysalis Education, 2003.

Look What You Can Make with Dozens of Household Items! by Kelly Milner Halls. Honesdale, PA: Boyds Mills Press, 2003.

Panda Bear, Panda Bear, What Do You See? by Bill Martin Jr. and Eric Carle. New York: Henry Holt Company, 2011.

Recycle Every Day! by Nancy Elizabeth Wallace. Tarrytown, NY: Marshall Cavendish, 2006.

The New 50 Simple Things Kids Can Do to Save the Earth by Earthworks Group. Riverside, NJ: Andrews McMeel Publishing, 2009.

Where Have All the Pandas Gone? Questions and Answers About Endangered Species by Melvin Berger, Gilda Berger, and Jim Effler. New York: Scholastic Press, 2001.

Why Should I Recycle? by Jen Green. Hauppauge, NY: Barron's Educational Series, 2005.

References

Alliance for Service Learning in Education Reform (ASLER). Standards of Quality for School-Based Service Learning. *Equity and Excellence in Education*, 26, no. 2 (1993): 71–73.

American Association for the Advancement of Science. *Science for All Americans*. Washington, DC: AAAS, 1989.

Anderson, J. B., and D. Hill. "Principles of Good Practice for Service Learning in Preservice Teacher Education." In J. B. Anderson, K. J. Swick, & J. Yff, eds. *Service Learning in Teacher Education: Enhancing the Growth of New Teachers, Their Students, and Communities.* New York: American Association of Colleges for Teacher Education, 2001.

Association for Supervision and Curriculum Development. www.ascd.org.

Beal, C. R., A. Garrod, K. Ruben, T. L. Stewart, and D. J. Dekle. "Children's Moral Orientation: Does the Gender of Dilemma Character Make a Difference?" *Journal of Moral Education*, 26 (1997): 45–58.

Bodrova E., and D. J. Leong. *Tools of the Mind: The Vygotskian Approach to Early Childhood Education.* Upper Saddle River, NJ: Prentice Hall, 1996.

Bredekamp, S. *Developmentally Appropriate Practice in Early Childhood Programs Serving Children from Birth through Age 8.* Washington, DC: National Association for the Education of Young Children,1987.

Bredekamp, S., and C. Copple. *Developmentally Appropriate Practice in Early Childhood Programs: Revised Edition.* Washington, DC: National Association for the Education of Young Children, 1997.

Bringle, R. G., M. A. Phillips, and M. Hudson. *The Measure of Service Learning: Research Scales to Assess Student Experiences.* Washington, DC: American Psychological Association, 2004.

Bullough, R. V. Jr., and D. K. Stokes. "Analyzing Personal Teaching Metaphors in Preservice Teacher Education and a Means for Encouraging Professional Development." *American Educational Research Journal*, 31 (1994): 197–224.

Caine, R. N., and G. Caine. *Education on the Edge of Possibility.* Alexandria, VA: Association for Supervision and Curriculum Development, 1997.

Claus, J., and C. Ogden, eds. *Service Learning for Youth Empowerment and Social Change.* New York: Peter Lang, 1999.

Cole, A. L., and J. G. Knowles. "Shattered Images: Understanding Expectations and Realities of Field Experiences." *Teaching & Teacher Education,* 9 (1993): 57–71.

Curriculum Task Force of the National Commission on Social Studies. *Charting a Course: Social Studies for the 21st Century.* Washington, DC: National Commission on Social Studies in the Schools, 1989.

Czuba, C., and N. Page. "Empowerment: What Is It?" *Journal of Extension,* 37, no 5 (1999). From joe.org, 1999.

DeJong, L., and F. J. Groomes. "A Constructivist Teacher Education Program That Incorporates Community Service to Prepare Students to Work with Children Living in Poverty." *Action in Teacher Education,* XVIII, no. 2 (1996): 86–95.

Derman-Sparks, L. *Anti-Bias Curriculum: Tools for Empowering Young Children.* Washington, DC: National Association for the Education of Young Children, 1989.

DeVries, R., and B. Zan. *Moral Classrooms, Moral Children: Creating a Constructivist Atmosphere in Early Education.* New York: Teachers College Press, 1994.

Dewey, J. *Democracy and Education.* New York: The MacMillan Company, 1916.

_____. *Experience and Education.* New York: Collier Books, 1938.

Donahue, D. M. "Service Learning for Preservice Teachers: Ethical Dilemmas for Practice." *Teaching and Teacher Education,* 15 (1999): 685–695.

Donovan, M. S., and J. D. Bransford. "Introduction." *How Students Learn: History, Mathematics, Science in the Classroom.* Washington, DC: National Research Council, 2005.

Eyler, J., and D. Giles. *Where's the Learning in Service Learning?* San Francisco, CA: Jossey-Bass, 1999.

Fiske, E. B. *Learning in Deed: The Power of Service Learning for American Schools.* Battle Creek, MI: W.K. Kellogg Foundation, 2001.

Furco, A. "Issues of Definition and Program Diversity in the Study of Service Learning." In S. H. Billig and A. S. Waterman, eds. *Studying Service Learning: Innovations in Educational Research Methodology.* Mahwah, NJ: Lawrence Erlbaum Associates, 2003.

Gilligan, C. *In a Different Voice.* Cambridge: Harvard Press, 1982.

Goldstein, L. S. "The Relational Zone: The Role of Caring Relationships in the Co-Construction of Mind." *American Education Research Journal,* 36, no. 3 (1999): 647–675.

Goffin, S. G., and C. S. Wilson. *Curriculum Models and Early Childhood Education: Appraising the Relationships* (2nd ed.). Upper Saddle River, NJ: Merrill Prentice Hall, 2001.

Herrick, J. *Empowerment Practice and Social Change: The Place for New Social Movement Theory.* Prepared for the New Social Movement and Community Organizing Conference, Seattle, WA, 1995.

Hatch, J. A. "Assessing the Quality of Early Childhood Qualitative Research." In. J. A. Hatch, ed. *Early Childhood Qualitative Research.* New York: Taylor & Francis (2007): 223–245.

Honnet, E. P., and S. J. Poulen. *Principles of Good Practice for Combining Service and Learning: A Wingspread Special Report.* Racine, WI: The Johnson Foundation, Inc., 1989.

Howard, J. "Service Learning Research: Foundational Issues." In S. H. Billig and A. S. Waterman, eds. *Studying Service Learning: Innovations in Educational Research Methodology.* Mahwah, NJ: Lawrence Erlbaum Associates, 2003.

International Reading Association. *Literacy Development and Prefirst Grade.* Newark, DE: IRA, 1989.

Jacoby, B. "Service Learning in Today's Higher Education." In B. Jacoby & Associates, *Service Learning in Higher Education.* San Francisco, CA: Jossey-Bass Inc., 1996.

Jalongo, M. R., and J. P. Isenberg. *Exploring Your Role: A Practitioner's Introduction to Early Childhood Education.* Upper Saddle River, NJ: Merrill Prentice Hall, 2000.

Kagan, D. M. "Professional Growth Among Preservice and Beginning Teachers." *Review of Educational Research,* 62 (1992): 129–69.

Kahne, J., and J. Westheimer. "In the Service of What? The Politics of Service Learning." *Phi Delta Kappan,* 77, no. 9 (1996): 593–599.

Kamii, C., and R. DeVries. *Group Games in Early Education: Implications of Piaget's Theory.* Washington, DC: The National Association for the Education of Young Children, 1980.

Katz, L., and S. Chard. *Engaging Children's Minds.* Norwood, NJ: Ablex, 1989.

Kaye, C. B. *The Complete Guide to Service Learning: Proven, Practical Ways to Engage Students in Civic Responsibility, Academic Curriculum, and Social Action.* Minneapolis, MN: Free Spirit Publishing, 2010.

Kendall, J. C., ed. *Combining Service and Learning: A Resource Book for Community and Public Service.* Vol. II. Raleigh, NC: National Society for Internships and Experiential Education, 1990.

Kilpatrick, W. H. *Remaking the Curriculum.* New York: Newson & Co., 1936.

King Jr., M. L. *The Purpose of Education.* The King Research and Education Institute, 1947.

Kinsley, C. W. "Service Learning: A Process to Connect Learning and Living." *Service Learning Bulletin,* 1997.

Kohlberg, L., and R. L. Selman. *Preparing School Personnel Relative to Values: A Look at Moral Education in the Schools.* Washington, DC: ERIC Clearinghouse on Teacher Education, 1972.

Lake, V. E., M. E. Vives, and I. Jones. "Preservice Teachers' Struggle to Transfer Metacognitive Processes from Their Integrated Mathematics and Science Methods Classes to Their Field Classrooms." *Journal of Early Childhood Teacher Education,* 24, no. 3 (2004): 181–187.

Lascarides, V. C., and B. F. Hinitz. *History of Early Childhood Education.* New York: Falmer Press, 2000.

Lewis, B. *What Do You Stand For? For Kids: A Guide to Building Character.* Minneapolis, MN: Free Spirit Publishing, 2005.

Lickona, T. *Educating for Character: How Our Schools Can Teach Respect and Responsibility.* New York: Bantam Books, 1991.

Lloyd-Jones, R., and A. A. Lunsford, eds. *The English Coalition Conference: Democracy Through Language.* Urbana, IL: National Council of Teachers of English, 1988.

Miles, M. B., and A. M. Huberman. *Qualitative Data Analysis: An Expanded Sourcebook* (2nd ed.). Thousand Oaks, CA: Sage, 1994.

National Association of Elementary School Principals. "NAESP Mission Statement and Goals" (2003–2006). From naesp.org.

National Council of Teachers of English. "On Reading, Learning to Read, and Effective Reading Instruction: An Overview of What We Know and How We Know It" (2004). From ncte.org.

National Council of Teachers of Mathematics. *Curriculum and Evaluation Standards for Mathematics.* Reston, VA: NCTM, 1989.

_____. *Professional Standards for Teaching Mathematics.* Reston, VA: NCTM, 2000.

National Research Council. *How People Learn: Bridging Research and Practice.* Washington, DC: National Research Council, 1999.

_____. *How Students Learn: History, Mathematics, and Science in the Classroom.* Washington, DC: National Research Council, 2005.

Paratore, C. *26 Big Things Small Hands Do.* Minneapolis, MN: Free Spirit Publishing, 2008.

Piaget, J. *The Moral Judgment of the Child.* (M. Gabain, Trans.). New York: A Free Press, 1965. (Original work published in 1932.)

Roberts, P., and A. Yang. *Kids Taking Action: Community Service Learning Projects, K–8.* Turners Falls, MA: Northeast Foundation for Children, 2002.

Sabin, E. *The Giving Book: Open the Door to a Lifetime of Giving.* New York: Watering Can Press, 2004.

Shoemaker, A. *Teaching Young Children Through Service: A Practical Guide for Understanding and Practicing Service-Learning with Children Ages 4 through 8.* St. Paul, MN: National Youth Leadership Council, 1999.

Shulman, L. S. "Those Who Understand: Knowledge and Growth in Teaching." *Educational Researcher,* 15 (1986): 4–14.

Smith, M. K. "Introduction to Informal Education." *The Encyclopedia of Informal Education* (2003). From infed.org/i-intro.htm.

Swick, K. J. "Service Learning in Early Childhood Teacher Education." *Early Childhood Education Journal,* 27, no. 2 (1999): 129–137.

Underhill, R. "Integrating Math and Science: We Need a Dialogue." *School Science and Mathematics,* 95 (1995): 225.

Verducci, S., and D. Pope. "Rationales for Integrating Service Learning in Teacher Education." In J. B. Anderson, K. J. Swick, & J. Yff (eds.), *Service Learning in Teacher Education: Enhancing the Growth of New Teachers, Their Students, and Communities.* New York: American Association of Colleges for Teacher Education, 2001.

Vygotsky, L. S. *Mind in Society.* Cambridge, MA: Harvard University Press, 1978.

Wade, R. C., and J. B. Anderson. "Community Service Learning: A Strategy for Preparing Human Service-Oriented Teachers." *Teacher Education Quarterly,* 23, no. 4 (1996): 59–74.

Weber, E. *Ideas Influencing Early Childhood Education: A Theoretical Analysis.* New York: Teachers College, Columbia University, 1984.

White, B. Y., and J. R. Fredrickson. "Inquiry, Modeling, and Metacognition: Making Science Accessible to All Children." *Cognition and Instruction,* 16, no. 1 (1998): 3–118.

Wellman, H. M. *The Child's Theory of Mind.* Cambridge, MA: MIT Press, 1990.

Yager, R., and M. Litz. "Integrated Science: The Importance of 'How' Versus 'What.'" *School Science and Mathematics,* 94 (1994): 338–346.

York, S. *Roots and Wings: Affirming Culture in Early Childhood Programs.* St. Paul, MN: Red Leaf Press, 1991.

Index

About the Authors

Vickie E. Lake, Ph.D., is an assistant professor of early childhood education in the Jeannine Rainbolt College of Education at the University of Oklahoma. A former teacher, staff developer, and early childhood district coordinator, Vickie has a passion for character education and high-quality education for young children. She has written for the *Journal of Early Childhood Teacher Education* and *Childhood Education,* among other publications, and presents at professional conferences. She lives in Tulsa, Oklahoma.

Ithel Jones, Ed.D., is an associate professor of early childhood education at Florida State University. Ithel was a teacher and primary school principal in his native Wales, and he has been a teacher educator for three universities in the United States. He currently teaches graduate and undergraduate courses in early childhood education and has published more than 30 articles and book chapters. He lives in Tallahassee, Florida.

Other Great Books from Free Spirit

Teaching Kids to Be Confident, Effective Communicators
For educators, grades K–6. 240 pp., softcover, 8½" x 11"

The Complete Guide to Service Learning
For educators, grades K–12. 288 pp., softcover, 8½" x 11"